Mr and Mrs Philip Caldwell

Selamat Datang

Ford Malaysia
February, 1982

jalan-jalan*

* **jalan-jalan,** n., & v.i. **1.** Pl. of *jalan* (also *jalan2*), roads, streets. **2.** v.i. Stroll, ramble, travel pleasurably without specific destination or goal in mind; hence travelling for the sake of the experience. [Pop. usage f. Malay *jalan* road]

PLATE FORTY-SIX

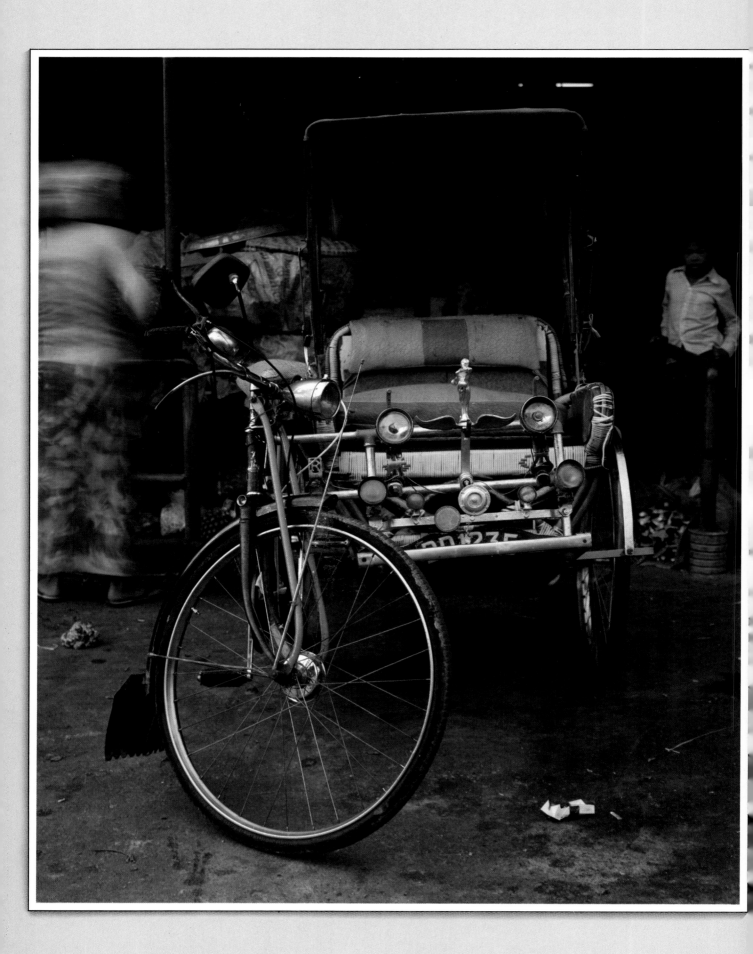

jalan-jalan

IMAGES OF MALAYSIA

Created and photographed by Hans Hoefer
Written by Peter Hutton

Produced by Apa Productions for
TOURIST DEVELOPMENT CORPORATION, MALAYSIA
1981

Produced by Apa Productions (Hong Kong) Ltd
for Tourist Development Corporation, Malaysia
First edition 1981
Photographs © 1981 TDC, Malaysia

Printed in Singapore by Koon Wah Printing (Pte) Ltd.

ISBN 9971-941-88-0

Contents

Note: Plate numbers and page numbers do not correspond: plates are numbered in the sequence in which they were photographed. The text describing each plate, beginning on page 180, is arranged in order of plate numbers with a cross reference to the relevant page number.

Foreword

This is a picture book about Malaysia. It is also a personal travel diary, a record of images that have captured my imagination as symbols of the country's varied and elusive soul.

Ten years ago I travelled to every accessible corner of Malaysia by nearly every means available — by train, car, bus, trishaw, raft, boat, aircraft and on foot. The result then was several thousand 35-millimetre transparencies, an illustrated guidebook, and a feeling that next time I might do it somewhat differently, though I wasn't sure when "next time" would happen, nor the form it would take.

In the years that followed, I visited Malaysia many times on various assignments. Two things emerged from these trips. I continued to discover just how accessible Malaysia's areas of interest really are, an accessibility enhanced across the country by a string of comfortable hotels and delightful old colonial-style guest houses (or "rest houses", as they are known locally); and, as my involvement with the land and its people increased, so too did my desire to cover it, photographically, in a way that had never been done before.

Nine years after my first memorable encounter with Malaysia, two seemingly unrelated purchases told me that "next time" had arrived. I had been riding motorcycles almost since the time I could walk; and I had used large-format plate cameras. I loved them both. In a joyous burst of self-indulgence, I bought a 1,000 cc BMW motorcycle from West Germany and a Deardorff eight-inch-by-ten-inch plate camera from the United States. Both were the best of their kind. Big bike. Big camera. Now I felt equipped to face the challenge of Malaysia.

For it *was* a challenge. How could the essence of a country of such physical, racial and cultural diversity be summed up in little more than one hundred pictures? Should I, as a professional photographer and designer, be looking for the pretty but predictable tropical beach at sunset with coconut palms or the equally picture-postcard scene of happy, smiling villagers? Should I be looking at the content of the photograph ("a picture is worth a thousand words"), or at its purely graphic elements ("art for art's sake")? Was I trying to produce an extended travel brochure, a book for other photographers to linger over, or a serious study with all sorts of deep insights into a country and its people. My goal was to realise aspects of all three approaches, and my knowledge of Malaysia was such that I knew where I wanted to go and why I wanted to go there. It was not a matter of chance, but of deliberate choice and selection.

That was one side of the film, so to speak. The other was even more professionally challenging. With the small-format Leicas I've used on other Asian assignments over the last fourteen years I've literally been able to shoot from the hip. And fast. Bang, bang, bang! Catching an instant of action. Freezing rapid movement. View, focus, click! Change of lens? A matter of seconds. Blast off an entire roll of film on a single subject? Of course!

Eight-by-ten just doesn't work that way. One sheet of Kodak Ektachrome eight-by-ten film is equal in area to sixty-one 35-millimetre images, and costs about the same as two rolls of standard small-format slide film. One shot, and the camera has to be reloaded — there's no room for mistakes or the luck of chance. The viewing screen gives an upside-down picture, and you can't see anything on it unless you duck under the suffocatingly hot viewing hood. The setting-up time (opening and mounting the camera body on the tripod, arranging focus and depth of field, checking light readings, sliding in the film-holder) takes an average of fifteen minutes; it could, depending on the subject, take up to an hour. And after all that, the shutter speeds are often agonisingly slow. It's impossible to catch a bird on the wing, a wave in mid-splash.

There were also some obvious limitations on subject matter. "People shots" tended to be informally formal rather than candid

— though everyone reveals aspects of personality even in the most formal pose. Strongly graphic subjects were natural candidates. Animate landscapes and inanimate man-made objects posed superbly — if the light was right!

The results can be seen in the following pages. Inevitably, there are omissions. More importantly, I think that a certain point of view comes across. These pictures are perceptions of Malaysia seen with a deep love and respect for the country and its people. They are the perceptions of a non-Malaysian, and perhaps have a less-than-predictable strength for that reason. They include pictures made with a mind to photography as a graphic art (though the images have a uniquely Malaysian flavour). They are also a visual celebration of one man's odyssey, of the joys and delights to be discovered on the road in Malaysia.

Some of these delights, regrettably, were unphotographable. Like arriving in a tiny seaside village (or just about anywhere else, for that matter) on a bike that dwarfed the small Hondas and Yamahas and Suzukis ridden by so many people in Malaysia. At such a moment, I always felt like a circus coming to town: hordes of eager admirers, dozens of questions, gasps of incredulity. Act two, of course, was setting up the camera — reactions to that alone made the journey worthwhile.

As the Malaysians say, "Have a good trip, and let's hope we meet again."

Selamat jalan, dan berjumpa lagi

Hans Hoefer

PLATE SIXTEEN

"Will the real Malaysia please stand up?"

What *is* Malaysia? Is it more or less than the sum of its parts? Promotional brochures offer one side of the reality: a land of golden beaches, crystal seas and mop-headed coconut palms, the domain of ancient empires, *satay,* primaeval jungles, an intricate culture, spectacular butterflies, and the *orang utan.*

There are also the bald facts. Born on 31 August 1957 as the sovereign Federation of Malaya, and enlarged on 16 September 1963 with the addition of the "Borneo territories" and a change of name, Malaysia today comprises in Peninsular (formerly West) Malaysia the states of Perlis, Kedah, Pulau Pinang (including Province Wellesley), Perak, Selangor, Melaka, Negeri Sembilan, Johor, Pahang, Trengganu and Kelantan; and in Borneo, the states of Sarawak and Sabah. It shares borders with Thailand, Singapore and Indonesia, and occupies a land area of 333,000 square kilometres between latitudes $1\frac{1}{2}°$ and $7°$N, of which roughly 200,000 square kilometres lie in the northern reaches of the world's third largest island, Borneo. The setting is equatorial, the vegetation lushly tropical, the climate hot and humid.

The nation is a constitutional monarchy, with the Yang di-Pertuan Agung (elected by his brother State rulers) as head of state. It is governed by an elected parliament headed by a prime minister. The population in 1980 was some 14,000,000, consisting of approximately 54 percent ethnic Malays and indigenous Borneo peoples, 35 percent Chinese, 10 percent Indians and 1 percent "others".

But there are other sides, other realities.

Seen from the window of an aircraft approaching the capital, Kuala Lumpur, the land appears smudged with the fingerprints of giants, a pattern of whorls, of circles within circles, laid down on a series of undulating hills stretching to a lumpy, hazy blue horizon; a Hampton Court maze on a scale beyond the mind's grasp. Here and there the fabric of the maze is pierced by a Cyclopean eye, an iris of milky green rimmed by greyish-white; in the centre, a silver pupil glinting in the sunlight. Farther afield, a great ochre scar, worn proudly like a battle wound; a bright medal on the uniform of jungle green and black.

The whorls of rubber and oil palm plantations, the eyes of tin-mining pools, the scars as more and more land is opened up for development: these are among the physical characteristics of Malaysia today. A century ago, they barely existed, for the exploitation of the country's natural resources and potential wealth had hardly begun. Fields of *padi,* in every shade of green, counterpaned the alluvial plains of the northwest and northeast, but the rice they produced was for internal consumption, not for export.

Small lodes of tin had long been worked in Perak, and since the 1850s miners living in crude bamboo-and-thatch huts had sluiced and washed for precious ore at Ampang near the muddy confluence — *kuala lumpur* — of the Klang and Gombak rivers in Selangor. The commercial prospects of *Hevea brasiliensis,* the Brazilian rubber tree, were still a dream in the mind of Henry "Rubber" Ridley. West African oil palm had another fifty years to wait before its economic impact would be felt in Malaysia. The jungle's canopies shaded most of the land, regal green parasols protecting a dormant monarch from the equatorial sun.

The tidy rural landscape now bordering many of Malaysia's trunk roads is still little more than a border. Beyond lie the riverine swamps, the heavily wooded hills and inaccessible mountains. But it is this ordered landscape of rubber trees, oil palm, *padi* and (not so beautiful) tin mines that the stranger is most likely to see at first glance; a glance revealing what is still the nation's major source of wealth. One side of the coin. But is it the *real* Malaysia?

PLATE FORTY-ONE

PLATE TWO

PLATE EIGHT

PLATE ONE

PLATE THIRTY-TWO

PLATE SEVENTY-NINE

PLATE TWENTY

PLATE THIRTY-FOUR

"Give me the simple life."

The idyll sought in the South Pacific by nineteenth-century European romantics (and happened upon by some, like Robert Louis Stevenson and Paul Gauguin) can be found now, and will be found tomorrow, in rural Malaysia. The ingredients? In economic terms, the small self-supporting village or *kampung,* blessed with fertile soil (providing rice or tapioca as dietary staples); an abundance of fruits (placating the sweet tooth while also supplying Vitamin C); and a seemingly self-perpetuating flow of useful raw materials (bamboo for building houses and making kitchen utensils, rattan and other canes used in furniture and basketware, assorted palms and grasses for thatch and weaving, coconuts for fuel, oil, water, milk and meat, and a variety of aromatic herbs to enliven the *kampung* cuisine or be used in traditional but remarkably effective medicinal applications.

In terms of a lifestyle, the idyll is no less real, no less appealing. The pace is gentle, relaxed. There are no dramatic seasonal changes to mark the slow progression through one year to the next, and were it not for the heavier-than-usual rains brought in by the southwest and northeast monsoon winds it would be difficult to say where one year ended and another began — no autumn leaves, no branches etched against a wintry sky. How does rural Malaysia perceive the passing of time?

Annual festivals, most of them based on a lunar calendar, are part of the answer. For Muslims (and that includes all Malays) one of the year's highlights is the celebration of Hari Raya Puasa at the end of Ramadan, the month of *puasa* or fasting; for the Chinese, it is the fifteen days between the beginning of the lunar New Year and Chap Goh Meh; for Hindu Indians, it is Deepavali, the "festival of lights". All such times are an occasion for "spring cleaning", for the painting of homes and the buying of new clothes, for gift-giving, for visiting friends and relatives — and especially for family reunions (the extended family of parents, grandparents, aunts, uncles and a thousand cousins is still a vital part of the life of most Malaysians).

There is also *musim buah,* the "fruit season". In fact, there are several "fruit seasons", though the casual observer could be excused for thinking of Malaysia as a year-round cornucopia of luscious tropical offerings. With some fruits, this is true. But mangosteens and rambutans, *buah duku* and *langsat,* among others, all have their appointed time — and none creates greater anticipation, or sets so many mouths a-watering, than the durian, whose spiky exterior enshrines a taste adventure defying description ("creamed custard laced with garlic" is one of the better of many attempts to pin down its elusive, addictive richness).

Harvest cycles also establish patterns within the year. Or used to, for the introduction of new strains of rice and the opening up of new irrigation systems (particularly in the northwest of Peninsular Malaysia) has made two or even three annual crops possible.

But back home in the *kampung,* life's pleasures remain essentially simple and undemanding. Ladies of the household take pride in their cleaner-than-clean yard (even the dust is dusted spotless). Buffaloes doze in muddy wallows in a nearby paddy. Children and chickens and young goats scamper and scatter to the sound of pestles pounding spices in stone mortars. The grounds of the small mosque are alive with colourful *baju* and sarongs as men gather for Friday prayers. A special event — a wedding, the end of a harvest season — and there might be a performance of *wayang kulit* (leather-puppet shadow plays) or traditional dances. But every day, come evening, it's time to slip out of workaday clothes, wrap yourself in a sarong, and relax with a game of checkers... or just talk.

It may not be a rich life. Nevertheless, its tangible harmony and happiness are very real facets of Malaysia. Not the whole gem, perhaps, but an aspect that cannot be ignored.

PLATE THREE

PLATE SEVEN

PLATE SIXTY-TWO

PLATE SEVENTEEN

The sea and its tributaries, the rivers, have profoundly influenced Malaysia's destiny. On the western coast of the peninsula, along the Straits of Malacca that separate it from Sumatra, sea-borne trade made the fifteenth-century Sultanate of Melaka "the richest seaport with the greatest number of merchants and abundance of shipping that can be found in the whole world" — so rich and desirable as an *entrepôt* that in 1511 it became the first victim of Portuguese expansion in the "East Indies"; and from across that same strait have come the ancestors of many of today's Malaysians (the state of Negeri Sembilan, especially, is populated largely by descendants of Minangkabau migrants from west Sumatra).

Off the eastern coast of the peninsula, and the northern and northwestern coasts of Borneo, the translucent turquoise waters of the South China Sea carried trading junks, emissaries and adventurers from China. Everywhere, sheltered harbours, bays and estuaries provided havens for fishing fleets — the coastal seas were a larder profusely stocked with fish, crabs, lobsters, prawns and squid; seafood (smoked, dried, steamed or fried) was, and remains, as much a part of the local diet as rice.

The coastal and riverine waterways were also highways. Until little more than a hundred years ago, Malaysia needed no road maps. Quite simply, there were no roads. There were crude tracks and pathways, a fragile spiderweb across the land, but that was all. Errands of mercy and trade were carried by *sampan, perahu* and raft, for the only villages and towns of any size sprouted along the banks of the rivers, huddled at river-and-ocean estuaries or clung like limpets to a patch of friendly coastline. To travel then was to travel by water.

A glance at any modern map of Malaysia reveals an abundance of towns and cities beginning with *kuala* — Kuala Lumpur, Kuala Trengganu, Kuala Kangsar, Kuala Lipis. They all have a feature in common: there is water at their front doorstep, be it the mouth of a river, an estuary, or the meeting of one or more streams (all of which meanings are embraced by *kuala*). For such towns and hamlets the river was a source of life — a meeting place for fishermen and inland traders, a communal bath-house, a natural site for a market. On the east coast of the peninsula, these were (and sometimes still are) the places to enjoy the adult pastimes of kite-flying and top-spinning.

Only in the last decades of the nineteenth century, when large-scale tin mining was truly under way and rubber plantations were beginning to blanket the countryside, did roads (and railways) start to play an important role in commerce and communications.

In more recent years, aeroplanes, diesel locomotives, long-distance trucks, hard-driven "out-station" taxis, private cars and mosquito-like clouds of zooming, screaming, ear-shattering Japanese motorcycles have made trade and human contact more easy in most areas. But they have never wholly supplanted the rivers and the sea in Malaysia's life, and it is doubtful that they ever will. Rafts of lashed bamboo continue to carry goods and people through otherwise inaccessible areas of Taman Negara (the National Park); fast, powerful motorboats link major towns along the coasts of Sarawak and Sabah; and similar craft are a lifeline to remote up-river settlements.

And the sea, always the sea. Spotted with islands of exquisite beauty: Tioman, Langkawi, Perhentian, Pangkor — the names alone are a siren's song, luring seafarers to paradise. Here is a coastline of long, deserted, golden beaches; bleached skeletons of shell and coral; underwater kingdoms offering more colour than the spectrum admits; groves of coconut palms and feathery casuarinas; aromas of salt air and drying fish; gay-prowed boats, stranded like sun-drenched lizards on hot sand above the tide-wrack — until tomorrow, when they take to the water. Another facet of Malaysia.

PLATE EIGHTY-THREE

PLATE FIFTY-THREE

PLATE EIGHTY-ONE

PLATE NINETY-SEVEN

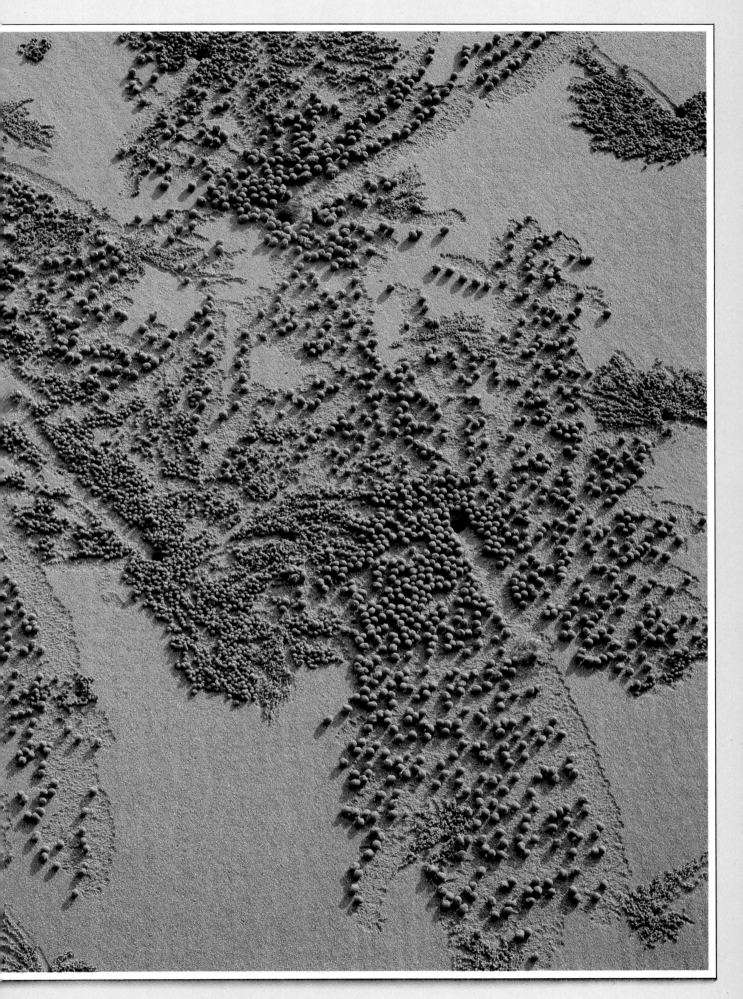

PLATE NINETEEN

PLATE EIGHTY-FOUR

PLATE TWENTY-TWO

PLATE NINETY-TWO

Another time, another place, in some ways almost a time warp; at the very least, a sudden jolting awareness (not unpleasant) that the apparent timelessness of rural, *kampung* Malaysia is counterpointed by a decidedly twentieth-century personality — the towns and cities.

The landscape through which you have been passing, be it oil palm or rubber estates, fields of *padi*, or small clusters of houses surrounded by fruit trees and bedecked with plants in brightly painted pots... this familiar territory suddenly gives way, with surprising speed, to a wide main street lined with two- or three-storey "shop-houses" (shop on the ground floor, living quarters above), often ornately decorated with stucco mouldings or colourful tilework. A shopkeeper's hoarding might proclaim "Syarikat Rahim Abdullah Sdn. Bhd.", though more likely (the Chinese being the currently dominant small traders and commercial entrepreneurs) it will be "Syarikat Boon Teng Wah"; illuminated signs carry the flowing, organic *jawi* Arabic script or the bold, squared-off brush strokes of Chinese characters limned in red.

Pavements, the *kaki lima* or "five-foot-way" covered arcades separating shopfront from street or storm-drain, are littered with an overflow of enticing riches spilling out from crowded shops. Every street corner seems to have its *kedai kopi*, the coffee shop serving food, refreshment and town gossip in equal parts — a bowl of *kway teow* noodles, a plate of *roti paratha* or *roti canai* (Indian bread or pancakes to be dipped in a thin curry), a dozen sticks of charcoal-grilled *satay* served with a spicy peanut-and-chilli sauce, all washed down with cups of *teh susu* or *kopi susu*, milky-sweet and bearing little resemblance to either tea or coffee; or it might be a glass of freshly pressed sugarcane juice or black, creamy-headed "Dog's Head" stout.

While many of Malaysia's small- to medium-sized towns have physical features in common, and while it is sometimes possible to travel through a town thinking "I've been here before" (when in fact you haven't), they all possess their own singular quality. Yong Peng, in Johor, surprises with its straight-up-and-down facades of weatherboard, almost like something from a Wild West movie; Kuala Lipis, in Pahang on the edge of Taman Negara, has a handful of "ladder streets" that wouldn't be out of place in Hong Kong. Nor, as the towns grow larger, is the transition from bucolic landscape to urban clutter quite so abrupt: Johor Bahru and Kuala Lumpur have their corridor suburbs, their burgeoning satellite towns-within-towns.

And there is *the* city, KL (nobody, but nobody, would ever use its full name). Brash, bustling, noisy, congested; a bewildering, infuriating maze of one-way streets. At the same time, one of Southeast Asia's more attractive cities, adorned with superb modern architecture (a delicious contrast with the colonial quaintness of the railway station, built — so rumour has it — to withstand the weight of a metre of snow on its minaretted Moorish roof!); vital, pulsating, filled with generous clamour; music caterwauling from night markets; the thump of piledrivers as yet another bank building rises to challenge the skyline; young office girls looking as though they've just stepped in from the Champs Elysées or Fifth Avenue.

KL. It is the grandeur and serenity of Masjid Negara, the National Mosque; the cacophonous, frenetic pace of Jalan Petaling, where sellers and buyers do business as though there were no tomorrow; *attap*-roofed foodstalls in the shadow of a highrise building housing a supermarket; tree roots grimly seeking a toe-hold in the cracked veneer of an old shop-house.

For even amid the modernity and discos, the trendy boutiques and restaurants, the green world is not far away...

PLATE SIXTY-SIX

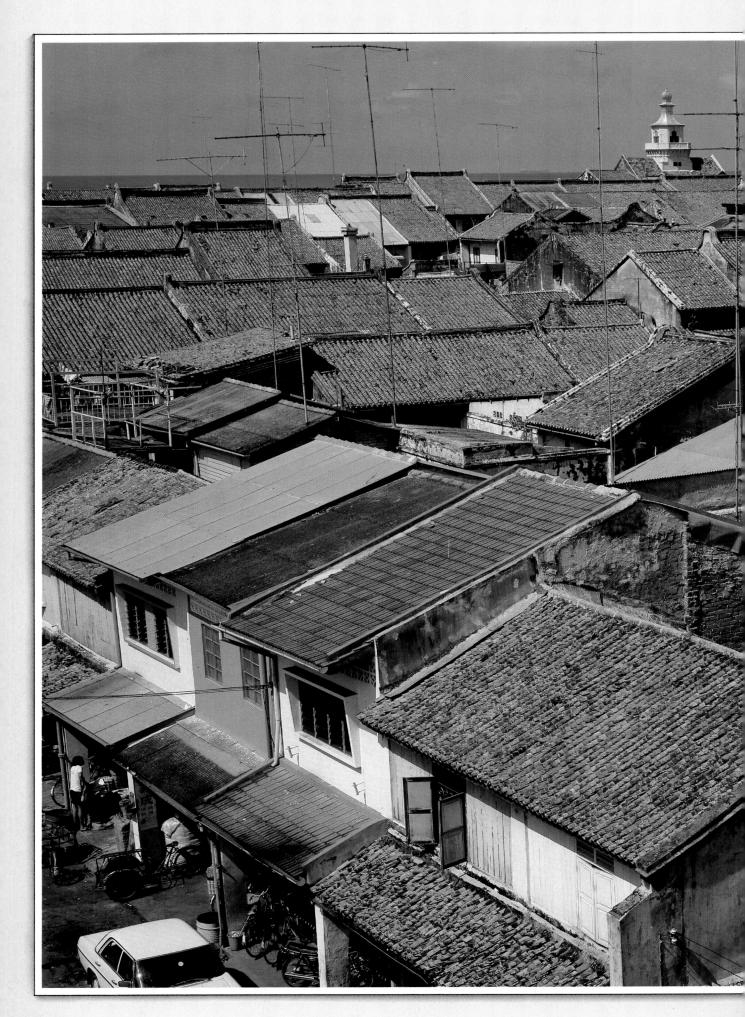

PLATE TEN

PLATE ELEVEN

111

PLATE FIFTY-FOUR

115

PLATE FIFTY-ONE

PLATE FORTY-EIGHT

PLATE NINETY-FOUR

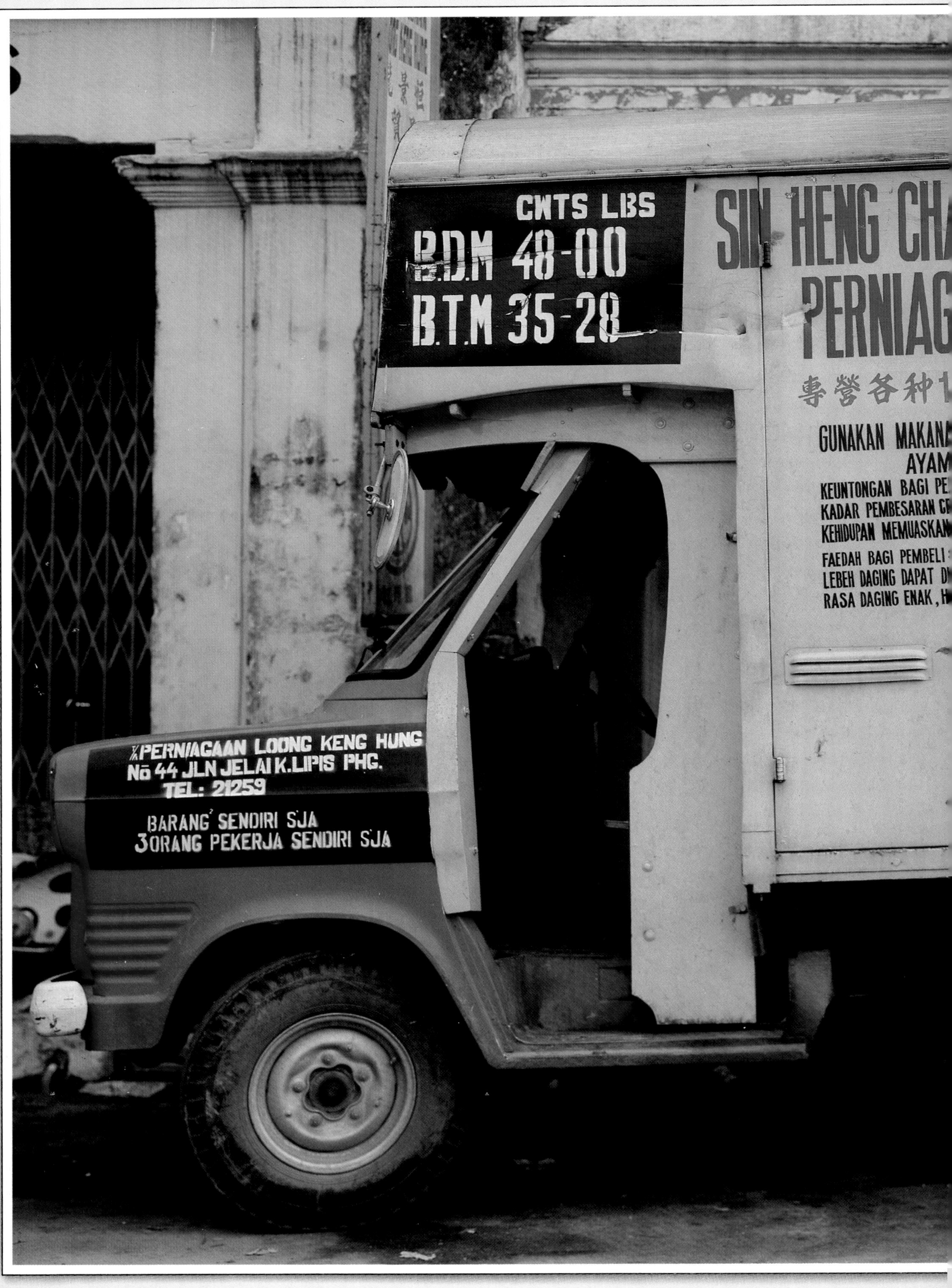

PLATE SEVENTY-SEVEN

PLATE NINETY-THREE

PLATE THIRTY

PLATE FORTY-FOUR

PLATE TWENTY-THREE

PLATE THIRTY-EIGHT

PLATE THIRTY-SIX

PLATE FIFTY-EIGHT

O nce upon a time (only hours ago, geologically speaking, but tens of millions of years before *Homo sapiens* made his appearance), the jungles of Malaysia were born. In origin and continuity, they are still the world's oldest, older by far than those of equatorial Africa or Brazil. Some of the jungle's inhabitants, too, are similarly ancient on the evolutionary scale: the pangolin or scaly ant-eater, a loveable relative of the armadillo, owes ancestral deference to no-one in the animal kingdom; the wild elephants (about three or four hundred) who roam the jungle fastness, and who sometimes create havoc in a hapless farmer's plot, are not exactly youngsters in hereditary terms; as for the insect world, it abounds with unlikely looking critturs whose family tree dates back to the carboniferous fossils some three hundred million years ago — with scarcely a change in looks!

So, it is an old jungle, with some old inhabitants. And with surprises, even for the most experienced adventurers. You're on the jungle floor, picking your way carefully through the tangle of vines and monstrous tree roots and thorns that make a surgeon's scalpel seem blunt; it is shadowy and humid, but not too hot. Suddenly, a gigantic reef of dead white coral rises in front of you. Underwater with Jungle Jim?

No. Just one of the many wind-and-water-etched cores of limestone that thrust upward through Malaysia's soil. They're soft and treacherous to climb, but some of their accessible caves have revealed signs of early habitation that could revolutionise the archaeology of man.

Contrary to popular belief, the true jungle is not difficult to traverse. Leafy canopies, as much as fifty metres above the ground, shield the soil from sunlight, and there is little scrubby vegetation to block your path. The rough stuff, a morass of impenetrable thickets and creepers, belongs to the secondary jungle... that's something else again, and Malaysia has plenty of it.

But where do the jungles begin? To the visitor's mind, in the garden outside the hotel — orchids, and large-leafed "things" that look ready to eat any stray pedestrian. Yes, there are carnivorous plants, happily munching on careless bugs and miniscule flying creatures. Within twenty kilometres of KL you can hear the eerie "whoop-whoop" cry of the gibbon; and there are tiger pad-marks to be seen up in the hills near Bentong. Small squirrels that rummage through suburban gardens, and occasional visitations by civet cats and pythons, are constant reminders of the jungle's proximity and fecundity.

It is a fragile ecosystem, and those jungle areas that have been cleared for crops or plantations might take a hundred years to revert to their natural state if left alone — *if* they revert at all. In some cases, clearance has produced an artificial beauty: rolling tea estates hugging the contours of the uplands; the famous hill stations once favoured by colonial officers as an escape from the heat of the plains; market gardens and flowerbeds rich in temperate-climate blooms (asters and marigolds and roses in the tropics!).

There are also the unsullied heights, none more spectacular than the stony folds and ridges of Sabah's Gunung Kinabalu, the tallest mountain in Southeast Asia.

It is a wondrous world, this Malaysian jungle. Unbelievably rich in epiphytic plants, parasites that sometimes strangle the tall, proud hardwood trees (though the numerous species we know as orchids produce exquisite blooms). The insect population is beyond counting, and is a goldmine for lepidopterists and other bug-catchers on the lookout for a Rajah Brooke (a glorious turquoise-and-black butterfly named after the first "White Rajah" of Sarawak) or a ten-centimetre-long horned rhinoceros beetle.

Of all Malaysia's natural and man-made attractions, the rain forest and the jungle are without doubt the most stunning, the most pervasive, the most memorable. From such landscapes, mankind is thought to have sprung... once upon a time.

PLATE ONE HUNDRED AND ON

PLATE NINETY-SIX

PLATE THIRTY-NINE

PLATE TWENTY-EIGHT

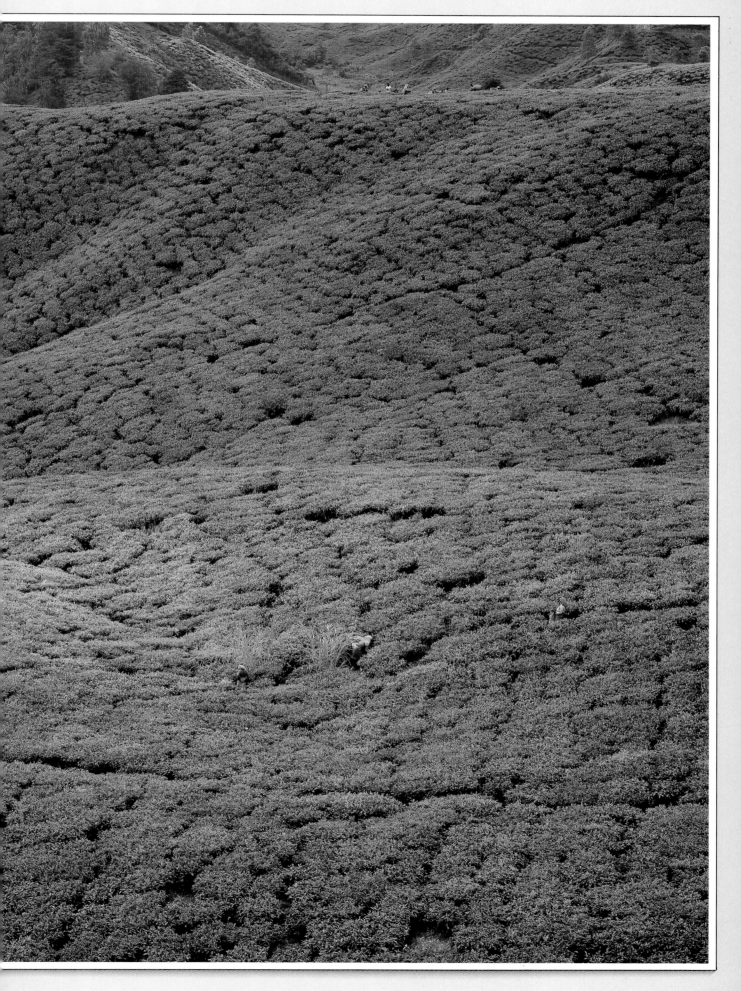

PLATE SEVENTY-SIX

PLATE TWENTY-NINE

PLATE ONE HUNDRED

PLATE ONE HUNDRED AND FOUR

PLATE ONE HUNDRED AND SIX

PLATE ONE HUNDRED AND SEVEN

PLATE ONE HUNDRED AND FIVE

Big bike. Big camera. See pages 204–205 for further details on going *jalan jalan* with an 8 × 10 plate camera.

A traveller's notes

Going *jalan-jalan* in a country of such gentle delights as Malaysia is its own reward. In towns that I think I know like the back of my hand, I suddenly come across a building or a face or an event that adds another dimension to my Malaysian memories; on a jungle road I'm entranced by a tree, a spray of ferns, a waterfall that would have Wordsworth on his knees. The arresting image might be a pastel-hued rural mosque, an Indian shrine dedicated to Shiva or blue-faced Krishna in the midst of a platoon of disciplined rubber trees, a Chinese temple brilliant with gold leaf and bright red calligraphy; or a long stretch of deserted beach, a fishing village apparently adrift on stilts, the wondrous colour and chaos of a town market. So many powerful impressions, so many memories, so much to capture on film — if I could.

Four factors controlled the shape of the book and my choice of subjects. First, the book had to represent Malaysia as a whole; second, the places visited should be generally accessible; third, "accessibility" did not mean being a whistle-stop on a major highway; and, four, the nature of the Deardorff camera. Each factor demands elaboration.

1. "Representative" Essentially this meant being aware of cultural, social, political and environmental issues — no bias toward beaches at the expense of the countryside, no favouring the visible culture of one racial group to the exclusion of another. Kuala Lumpur is extremely photogenic; but it appears in only eight of the one hundred and seven photographs reproduced here. Why? Because although KL is the financial, commercial and political centre of Malaysia, it is only a small part of the nation's overall day-to-day life. Just as important is the typical "coffee-shop corner" to be found in most Malaysian towns (PLATE 37, PAGES 92–93), the rural mosque (PLATES 42 & 49, PAGES 50–51), the riverine town (PLATE 60, PAGES 60–61). Personal preferences influenced many of my choices of subject, but they never overrode the essential pattern and character of the country.

2. "Accessible" Most of Malaysia's attractions are easy to get to (the peak of Gunung Kinabalu and the cathedral-like vastness of the Niah Caves are exceptions to this general rule, but it is impossible to ignore two of the country's outstanding natural sights). All of the coral-reef islands are within a few hours' boat-ride from the mainland; the peninsula's east coast beaches are alongside the highway or just minutes away from it. I did not include the interesting limestone caves in Kelantan and Trengganu because they're well off the beaten track; similarly, the pristine forest of Taman Negara (the National Park) is both remarkable and entrancing, but penetrable only by those with a taste for Tarzan-like adventure — it is not exactly territory for the pampered traveller!

3. "Main roads or back roads?" In Malaysia, as in most countries, roads were opened up to facilitate economic progress; in many cases, they partnered the growth of railways in the late nineteenth and early twentieth centuries, providing a lifeline for the engineers and labourers who undertook that often appallingly difficult task (take the train south from Kota Bharu to Kuala Lumpur, and the tenacity and courage of the men who laid steel tracks through this formidable terrain will be sure to impress you).

Commercial routes are not designed to reveal scenic beauty; they are more likely to take the path of least resistance (geographically speaking), and their attractions are a bonus rather than a deliberate goal. Such routes are invariably crowded with heavy traffic: logging trucks, oil tankers, interstate buses, out-station taxis and hordes of private cars — you spend more time watching the road than enjoying the passing scene.

I avoided trunk routes and highways whenever possible, preferring to take smaller, less busy roads that meander slowly through the landscape. I believe that part of the joy of travel is the travelling itself; there's more to it than simply arriving. Malaysia's back roads and byways amply reward this attitude, and I have seldom been disappointed by what I've found at the end of a ten- or twenty-kilometre jaunt down some inviting back-country lane. Along the east coast of the peninsula, in particular, if the road you're on is not actually hugging the seashore, just about any side road is likely to take you to a beautiful stretch of beach or a picturesque fishing village. "On the road in Malaysia" (PAGE 205) provides a few useful tips for motorcyclists and motorists who want to get the most out of their travels; though I hope that the photographs, and the descriptive text in this section, will encourage other travellers (Malaysians among them) to try a few out-of-the-ordinary itineraries, for the rewards are great.

4. "The camera" The idiosyncracies of 8 × 10 photography in the field are discussed on PAGES 204–205. Here, I merely want to mention those features that influenced my decisions on what to photograph.

It was impossible to be "invisible". That great lump of gear cannot be hidden or disguised. With a small 35-millimetre camera you can pretend that you're not really there; you're not conscious of imposing yourself on the lives of other people, and you can (if you're skilful) seem to blend into the background as you shoot candid portraits with a long lens or create exciting studies of a market with a wide-angle. With 8 × 10, you're not merely visible, you're the centre of everybody else's focus.

The 8 × 10 format was challenging and interesting for several reasons. On the one hand, it meant tremendous personal involvement — eye-to-eye contact. People were aware of being photographed, and could accept or reject the camera's presence. In accepting, they tended to project a self-image that was always

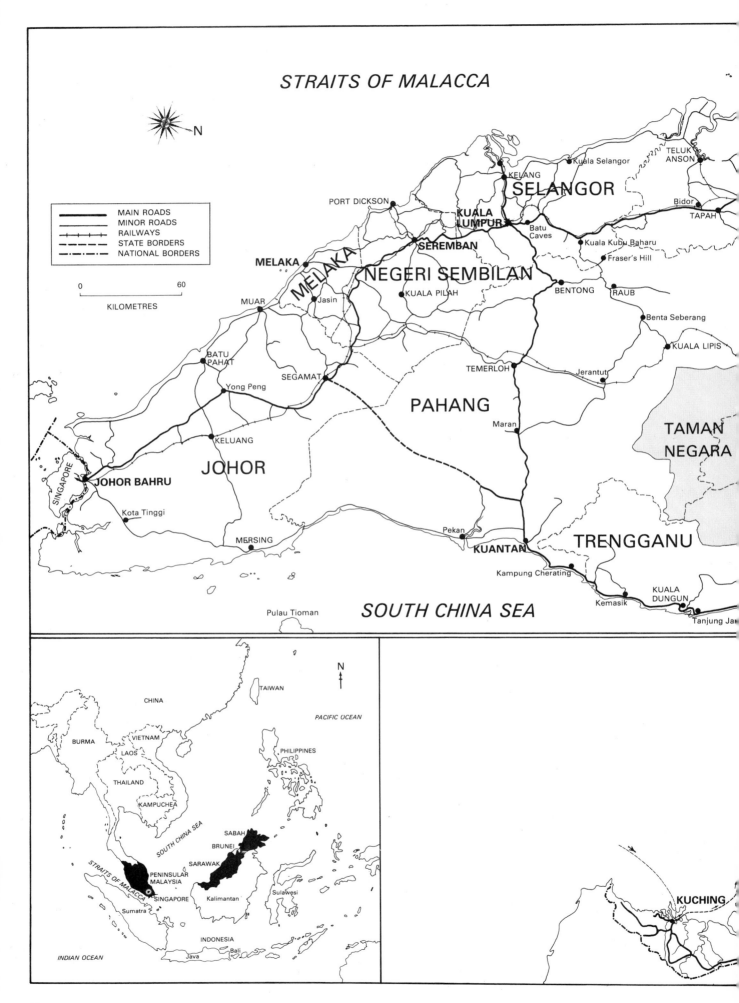

STRAITS OF MALACCA

SOUTH CHINA SEA

MAIN ROADS
MINOR ROADS
RAILWAYS
STATE BORDERS
NATIONAL BORDERS

0   60
KILOMETRES

SELANGOR

Kuala Selangor

TELUK ANSON

KELANG

Bidor

TAPAH

PORT DICKSON

KUALA LUMPUR

Batu Caves

Kuala Kubu Baharu

SEREMBAN

Fraser's Hill

MELAKA

MELAKA

NEGERI SEMBILAN

Kuala Pilah

BENTONG

RAUB

Jasin

Benta Seberang

MUAR

KUALA LIPIS

BATU PAHAT

TEMERLOH

Jerantut

Segamat

Yong Peng

PAHANG

TAMAN NEGARA

KELUANG

Maran

JOHOR

SINGAPORE

JOHOR BAHRU

Kota Tinggi

Pekan

TRENGGANU

MERSING

KUANTAN

Kampung Cherating

KUALA DUNGUN

Kemasik

Pulau Tioman

SOUTH CHINA SEA

Tanjung Ja

CHINA

TAIWAN

PACIFIC OCEAN

BURMA

VIETNAM

LAOS

PHILIPPINES

THAILAND

KAMPUCHEA

SOUTH CHINA SEA

SABAH

BRUNEI

SARAWAK

PENINSULAR MALAYSIA

SINGAPORE

Kalimantan

Sulawesi

Sumatra

KUCHING

INDONESIA

INDIAN OCEAN

Java

Bali

178

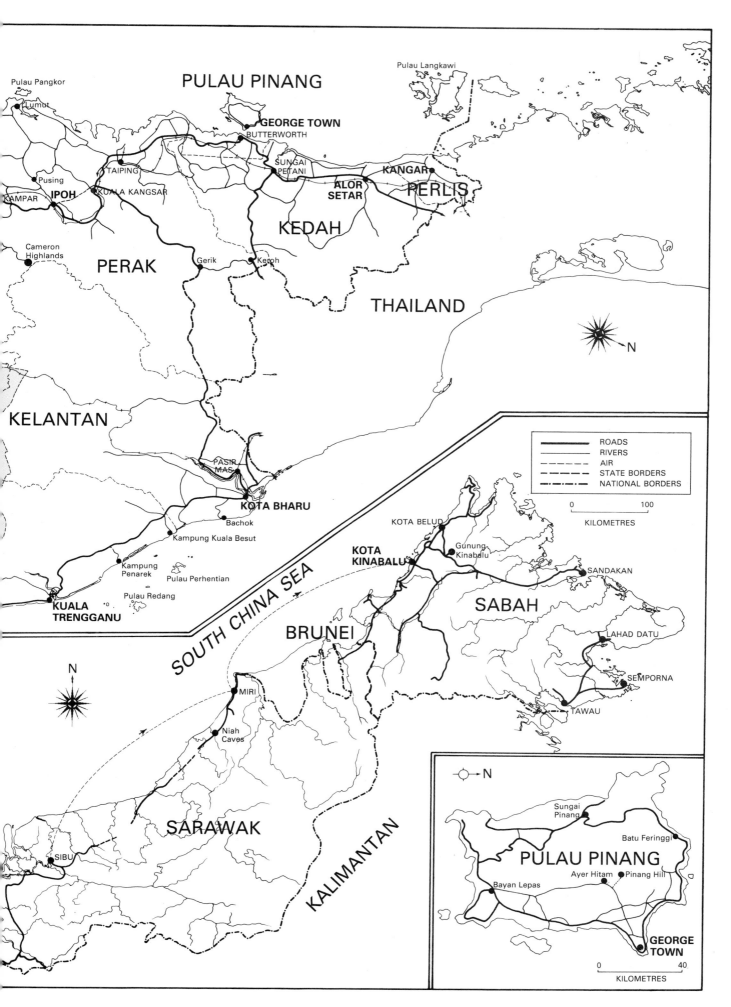

179

revealing, never dull; it was as though they were aware that a segment of their soul was being captured for eternity, and they became an integral part of a two-way process, photographer and subject involved and united in that moment of exposure.

Another point was that the large-format's sharpness of image could freeze tiny details that the roving eye might otherwise miss. The human eye is continually darting, shifting, moving, changing focus; it seldom rests long enough to register fine detail. An 8 × 10 image arrests such movement, almost forcing the eye into a concentration of visual capacity, an extreme awareness of small things, that so many of us leave behind as we leave childhood. Yet who doesn't become a child again, exploring the Ali Baba riches of the toyseller's wares in Sibu (PLATE 94, PAGES 120–121). And who, given this moment caught in time, can fail to notice the empty cigarette packet on the corrugated-iron awning, the implication that there are another one or two storeys above the frontage. This heightening of vision works in broader situations as well: tea-pickers sprinkled like multi-coloured grains of sugar across green highland slopes (PLATE 28, PAGES 158–159); cows being herded homeward by Indians at the foot of a hill smothered by womb-shaped Chinese graves (PLATE 31, PAGES 54–55).

The clarity and definition obtainable with 8 × 10 is, for me, like looking through an open window; nothing comes between the viewer and the subject, nothing inhibits the experience of seeing. This often makes me feel that I'm carrying an audience with me as I travel. I shoot not just what takes *my* fancy, but what I think will interest or surprise or delight my accompanying audience — I'm very conscious of them staring over my shoulder as I line up a shot.

Yet another factor involved in the choice of shots was the layout and format of the book itself. Not many

PLATES AND PAGES
In using this section to refer back to the plates, note that plate and page numbers do not correspond. The miniatures reproduced here are numbered in the order in which they were taken. To find any colour plate described in this text, turn to the page number or numbers printed at the bottom right of each miniature.

photographers enjoy the advantage of knowing how their photographs are going to be reproduced; you can spend a lot of time and imagination in framing what seems to be the perfect shot, only to discover on publication that some anonymous picture editor or art director has cropped it vertically (when you shot a horizontal) or has blown up a small detail that doesn't really make sense when taken out of context! Happily, with *jalan-jalan* I didn't have to contend with such problems.

I knew there would be roughly the same number of vertical pictures as there would be horizontals; and I knew that, with the exception of the section openings, there would always be two vertical pictures facing one another across the centre of a two-page spread, and that each horizontal would be used as a self-contained double-page spread. In most cases I envisioned the facing vertical pictures as being complementary, so I was always on the lookout for suitable "pairs" — hence, for example, the two sets of tiled steps near

Melaka (PLATES 4 & 18, PAGES 44–45) and the pair of patrician houses in Pinang (PLATES 57 & 56, PAGES 102–103).

As a result, of the three hundred sheets of film exposed in the course of my travels in Malaysia, probably two hundred and fifty *could* have been used in the book (thus doubling its size and its cost — there had to be a limit somewhere!). Those that survived the often painful selection process do, I hope, offer some unusual as well as predictable views of Malaysia. The "rejects" from *jalan-jalan* might, one of these days, find themselves between the covers of a book tentatively called *Satu empat jalan* — execrable colonial Malay which literally means "one four road" and thus, as a title, "One More for the Road".

The routes taken

The colour plates (PAGES 15–175) are arranged thematically in five sections: the land, the rural village, rivers and seashores, towns and cities, and the jungle, hills and mountains.

In this section, black and white miniatures of the colour plates are presented in the order in which they were photographed. The order follows four basic routes — three in the peninsula, and one in Sarawak and Sabah. Each route is recommended for the variety and different views of Malaysia that it provides; none, of course, has to be followed in the direction that I took. With Kuala Lumpur as your base (see the GENERAL MAP, PAGES 178–179), variations on routes north, south and east are easily devised or arranged; if you're coming to Malaysia through Singapore, the circuit from Johor Bahru up the east coast to Kuantan, westward across the mountains to KL and then down the west coast through Melaka makes a very attractive trip.

My four routes, as taken and photographed, were: **1.** Johor Bahru, Melaka, Port Dickson, Kuala Selangor, Teluk Anson, Cameron Highlands, Ipoh, Kuala Kangsar, Keroh, Alor Setar and Pulau Pinang (this itinerary skirts KL, though obviously you can take a break at the capital in any similar northbound or southbound journey); **2.** up the peninsula's east coast from Johor Bahru to Mersing, Pekan and Kuantan (from where you can continue north up the coast, or head cross-country to KL); **3.** Kuala Lumpur, Batu Caves, Fraser's Hill, Raub, Kuala Lipis, Kuantan, Kuala Trengganu and Kota Bharu; **4.** Kuching, Sibu, Miri, Kota Kinabalu and Gunung Kinabalu (this route, I need hardly add, was *not* done on a motorcycle).

More specific detail on each route is provided in the maps accompanying the text in this section.

Commentary on the plates

I should make it clear that I am a photographer and designer, not an agronomist, a professional historian or an expert on Malaysian culture (recommendations for further reading on such subjects are listed on PAGE 207).

As a result, many of the observations set down in this "diary" are quite personal, coloured by my experiences and preferences. They are also very close to the earth: I don't travel in an airconditioned limousine, I'm as much at home in a rambling old wooden guest house as I am in a modern luxury hotel, and I invariably eat local food in a *kedai kopi* (coffee shop) rather than seek out Western dishes; the latter are readily available in towns of any size, but if it comes to a choice between *wiener Schnitzel* and a bowl of *mee goreng* (fried noodles) liberally embellished with sliced chillies, I'll go for the noodles any time.

Because this is a photographic picture book, there are references to why a particular shot was chosen, or what happened while such-and-such a shot was being set up. These "happenings", sometimes quite amusing, helped turn an interesting journey into a series of delights.

PLATE 1   PAGES 24-25

Inside a rubber plantation on the way north from Johor Bahru to Muar — a scene impossible to miss when you're on the road in Malaysia.

The rubber tree is a native of Brazil, but for the last seventy years Malaysia has been the world's leading producer of natural rubber. The estates may cover hundreds or even thousands of hectares (these are the big ones, owned by state or joint-venture corporations); or they may consist of only a few hectares owned and tapped by one family.

This was a young plantation, perhaps ten or twelve years old — not so dense that overhead light was blocked out by heavy foliage. Plantations might *look* the same, but the light meter says they're not; some are so dark inside that a thirty-second exposure might be needed. This one, clean and open, needed only about one second, a fragment of time long enough to blur the bus. The bending of the trees is the result of prevailing winds, not lens distortion.

PLATE 2   PAGES 18-19

A *padi*-farmer just north of Muar. On his right, newly planted rice; on his left, a small field being ploughed and prepared for planting.

This became one of quite a number of unplanned shots. I found this stretch of cultivated land at about eight o'clock in the morning, a time still full of long shadows — a rare event in the tropics, for the sun gallops into the sky at dawn and hangs directly overhead most of the day.

The shot began as a landscape, with the farmer and his buffalo as soft-focus background features. By the time the Deardofff was mounted and set up, the farmer's curiosity had got the better of his natural reticence. He left his plough and came down to find out what this strange foreigner was doing. His coming forward (and a cigarette to help allay his suspicions) turned a landscape study into a portrait. Beautifully unpredictable, and certainly not anticipated. His proved to be the first of many similarly "accidental" portraits. Although I had a clear idea of the objects and places I wanted to photograph, I was entirely in the hands of Lady Luck when it came to people. It says a lot for the warm, cooperative nature of most Malay-

sians that very few turned down my requests to photograph them.

PLATE 3   PAGES 38-39

A typical "Malacca-style" *kampung* house between Muar and Melaka. Houses like this, generally set well back from the road, are among the most attractive to be found anywhere in Malaysia. Whitewash, natural timber and bright paintwork testify to great pride shown by householders in this area. The grounds of such houses are always trim and clean, while the interiors look as though they're dusted and polished on the hour, every hour.

PLATE 4   PAGE 44

A detail of the house shown in the preceding plate. The coloured tiles on the steps leading up to a spacious, open verandah are characteristic features of most rural houses around Melaka. This is a region that demands leisurely travel, partly as a preparation for the gentle pace of the town itself, and partly because there are so many pretty roadside vistas to be enjoyed. No matter how often I visit Melaka (and I've been there many times), I'm always sure to find something appealing to my photographer's fancy.

PLATE 5   PAGES 42-43

This house, with its steeply pitched roof of *attap* thatch, owes something to the traditional design of Minangkabau dwellings in west Sumatra, even though the gable ends do not turn upwards in the "buffalo horn" style. Open windows on all sides ensure that it is well ventilated and cool, even on the hottest days. The shot was easy enough to set up, but the lighting presented problems. It was about ten in the morning, and already the sun was very high. I had to make up my mind whether I wanted to expose for external detail — the roof and the yard — or for the detail within the shadowy area below the eaves. By choosing the latter, I had to accept that anything touched by direct sunlight would be slightly over-exposed.

PLATE 6   PAGE 41

A young girl living in the house had been watching me as I prepared for the general exterior shot. She was a little shy at first, but we got to talking over coffee, and she was soon happy to pose.

Where people were concerned, I never worked from a check-list that said "fisherman", "pretty *kampung* girl" or "typical farmer", but I took advantage of any opportunity that strolled up — which is about the closest you can get to spontaneity with 8 × 10.

Shortly before Melaka I took a semi-circular detour through the lovely countryside around Jasin. This house caught my eye for a couple of reasons: the child's tricycle and a plastic ball added a human touch, and the gaily painted flowerpots reflected the liking of many Malaysians for bold, strong colours. I'm sure that a lot of visitors from temperate zones are surprised by such an abundance of potted plants — why are they necessary, when an average *kampung* house is surrounded by perennially blooming frangipani, hibiscus and bougainvillaea (not to mention coconuts, bananas and a host of fruit-bearing trees)? The Malays are very house-proud, and that must have a lot to do with it; more practically, plants that can be individually cared for in pots have a better chance of survival than those that try to eke nutrition from the red laterite earth. Despite the country's apparent lushness, gardens in the "Western" style are very difficult to cultivate.

One commercial crop that has taken firm and profitable root in Malaysia's soil is the oil palm. The last twenty years, especially, have seen a tremendous growth in the number and size of oil palm plantations, for the end product (palm oil) is an essential ingredient in many soaps and cooking oils. This well-kept estate, near Jasin, is about fifteen years old, and will continue to be productive for many years to come, at least until the palms grow too tall for the clusters of blackish-orange nuts to be harvested by man or machine. The oldest oil palm in Southeast Asia (in the Bogor Botanic Gardens, Java), is as tall as a coconut palm, and still growing.

And so, on to Melaka (or Malacca, as it is better known to the outside world), one of my favourite towns, and a must for anyone interested in the history of the peninsula.

Although some details of its early history, as recounted in the ancient *Sejarah Melayu* ("Malay Annals"), are still debated by scholars, Melaka was apparently founded at the end of the fourteenth century AD by Parameswara, a fugitive prince from the declining Srivijaya empire in south Sumatra. The whole of Southeast Asia was then in turmoil. Amid surrounding chaos, Parameswara established a powerful city state and embraced Islam (several of modern Malaysia's royal families have proud links with the original "Malacca Sultanate"). The prince's new city flourished, its control of the Straits of Malacca also giving it control over the east- and westbound trade linking China and the fabled Spice Islands with India and the Persian Gulf. Gold, silks, porcelain and costly spices filled its warehouses, and it was said that more than a hundred languages were spoken in its marketplace as traders passed through from every corner of the Asian world. Then the West intervened.

In 1498, Vasco da Gama rounded the southern tip of Africa and opened a sea route to India. Portuguese trading posts sprang up in Calicut, Bombay and Goa. The next step, control of the spice trade, was undertaken in 1511 when Afonso d'Albuquerque besieged Melaka. Its fall, after seventeen days of bitter fighting, marked the beginning of three hundred and forty years of European domination.

Portuguese Melaka was taken by the Dutch in 1641. At the end of the eighteenth century the British assumed control, lost it a short time later, and regained it when they accepted Melaka from the Dutch in exchange for their own impoverished Sumatran base at

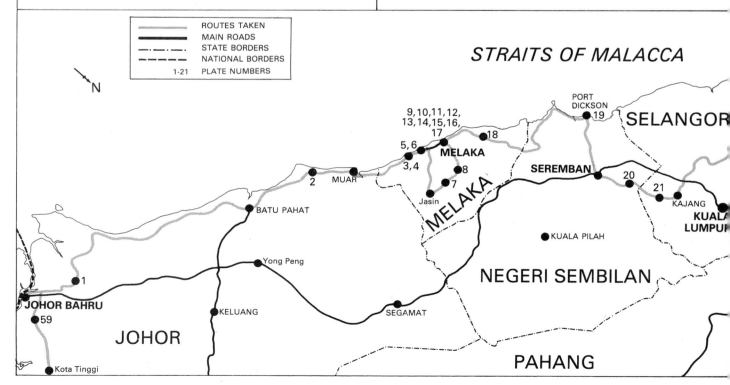

Bencoolen (modern Bengkulu) in 1824.

In the heart of old Melaka there are still buildings that evoke its romantic and often violent past. Around it, the new Melaka displays all the neon colour and noisy vivacity of a middle-sized, prosperous Malaysian town.

PLATE 9   PAGES 62-63

Most people begin their exploration of Melaka in the town square with its old, salmon-pink Dutch buildings. I prefer to start with the mouth of the river, on the southern (Muar) bank. I got here quite early in the morning, when the sky looked as if it had just been freshly washed, and was greeted by these sailing boats. They were inter-island traders from Sumatra, and it was easy to imagine similar scenes two or three hundred years ago — though I wonder whether the high spirits and friendliness of the crews would have been the same; I like to think so. I chose a small aperture and a slow shutter-speed (one-eighth of a second) so that some movement would blur.

The combination of the Deardorff and a tripod strong enough to support it without camera-shake is quite a heavy package — I don't carry it for fun. Nevertheless, Melaka's points of interest are so close together, and the atmosphere of the old town is so charming, that I never felt I was doing penance by wandering around with all that paraphernalia balanced on one shoulder. For anyone using a small-format camera (even with lots of accessories), Melaka is a walker's dream.

PLATE 10   PAGES 98-99

This seaward view of the old quarter was taken from the top of the *muezzin*'s minaret of a small, old mosque. If you ignore the cars, it is about as close as you can now get to an impression of how the town's mercantile enclave might have looked a century or more ago; most other high vantage points are marred by high-rise office blocks or apartment buildings.

I had asked at the mosque for permission to climb the minaret, and it was readily and politely granted. Up I went. The circular staircase was so narrow I could barely squeeze through. When I got to the top my field of view was limited by very narrow window slits. There was so little space I had one tripod leg against the wall, one a few steps down the stairs, and the other with nowhere to go at all. The *menara* was solidly built of brick, but a fierce wind convinced me that the whole tower must be moving. I braced the camera body against the wall, exposed at one-thirtieth of a second, and hoped for the best!

In exploring Melaka, in savouring the treasures held in its small but fascinating museum, I'm always impressed by the diversity of its historical and cultural heritage — and by Malaysia's as well. Many early European maps of East Asia referred to the peninsula as "Malacca" (doing justice to the Sultanate's extensive sway), but how well was it known before 1511? The peninsula was probably Ptolemy's Chersonese, and Chinese Buddhists making the pilgrimage to India by sea certainly knew of it by the fourth century AD. Long before Parameswara accepted Islam in about 1410, there had been Hindu states in the north of the country, and when the Malacca Sultanate was established, the town had been visited by Arab and Indian traders for centuries.

So Melaka and the peninsula were not exactly backwaters when an emissary from the Ming Emperor arrived with a fleet of eighteen junks in 1509. The ambassador was Admiral Cheng Ho, a famous

PLATE 11   PAGES 108-109

seafarer who visited Melaka on several occasions, and became something of a folk hero to Chinese immigrants. This temple, the Cheng Hoon Teng, was erected in his memory and is principally dedicated to Kuan Yin, the Buddhist Goddess of Mercy. Dating in part from about 1650, it is the oldest Chinese temple in the country.

Behind the main hall is a room containing rows of ancestor tablets, memorials to those dead and those yet to die. Filial piety and respect for elders

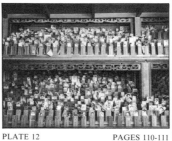

PLATE 12   PAGES 110-111

and parents have had a powerful influence on Chinese society for several thousand years. I hadn't the space to play around with bellows and tilt, but I wanted maximum depth of field, so this shot was taken at a minimum aperture of f/64 and an exposure of about four minutes.

PLATE 13   PAGE 112

This striking statue, lovingly cared for and adorned with finery, is in the Cheng Hoon Teng temple. The bold colours of the robes and the ornate headdress are typical of those favoured by the Chinese, with vermilion and gold both being regarded as colours of good omen and fortune.

The statue, deep in the heart of the temple, is softly lit by diffused, almost shadowless light, and a small aperture and long exposure were necessary.

(Places of worship are among Malaysia's more photogenic subjects; however, if you want to shoot interiors or worshippers, always ask for permission first.)

Considering the great power it once wielded, old Melaka covers a surprisingly small area. This, today, is part of its mellow charm, for its highpoints can all be seen easily in the course of a day's relaxed strolling. Apart from the Stadhuys, the old churches and the Porta de Santiago (St James' Gate, all that remains of

PLATE 14   PAGE 100

PLATE 15   PAGE 101

the Portuguese fortress), a favourite place with visitors is Jalan Gelanggan (formerly Jonker Street), where antique and curio shops stand alongside lovely houses like this one. Really fine antiques are hard to come by in Melaka now (though anyone interested in porcelain will be attracted by the delicate Nonya ware with its finely flowered patterns in pale pink, rose, mauve and lime green), but the superbly carved doors and stucco decor of the houses along Jonker and Heeren Streets should more than compensate for any disappointment you might feel at not finding a rare collector's item.

It would be possible to devote an entire photographic book to Melaka houses. Unfortunately, I had to make do with just one — a difficult task, with such a wealth of beauty and fascinating detail to choose from. This house is typical of the style.

The Melaka edifice longest in continuous use is the large, rambling Stadhuys or town hall. Built in stages between 1641 and 1660, its massive castle-like walls still contain government offices. An imposing broad staircase leads from the town square to what used to be the governors' apartments, and the past becomes almost

PLATE 16   PAGES 10-11

tangible as you climb upwards. But even more intriguing, for me, are the bolted doors and stairway that face the square a little nearer to the eighteenth-century Christ Church.

This shot was taken after sunset, in rapidly fading twilight. When I first opened the shutter, the correct exposure time was eight minutes, but because the light was disappearing extremely fast I had to estimate further exposure time to take into account the loss of light. Such a long exposure accumulates available light (even though the sky was deep violet, almost black, there was *some* light still there), but produces a slight colour shift.

Malaysia's oldest Chinese cemetery (and the largest outside of China) is Bukit China, a prominent hill on the edge of old Melaka. I was exploring it, looking for a good subject, when I discovered this small

PLATE 17   PAGES 52-53

Muslim graveyard near the foot of the hill. I was there just before Ramadan, the Muslim fasting month, and some of the gravestones had been freshly painted to identify the resting places of particular families or relatives. Muslims traditionally visit graveyards during Ramadan, and especially on Hari Raya Puasa, the day of celebration that marks the end of the fast. A man's burial site is marked by round stone pillars, a woman's by flat-sided stones.

The attractive coastline north of Melaka is dotted here and there with comfortable, inexpensive hotels that were once private mansions. Here too there are

PLATE 18   PAGE 45

more examples of the rich tilework so reminiscent of that found in parts of Portugal. The gently curving balustrades, the use of half-moon fanlights above shop-house windows and doorways, the applied plaster swags of fruit and flowers decorating the facades of so many old homes and shops throughout Malaysia — these all seem to owe a considerable debt

to Portuguese architectural styles, and are graphic reminders of the enormous influence enjoyed by Melaka in earlier days.

I continued north along the coast to Blue Lagoon and Port Dickson, a beach resort area that has been popular for more than half a century. It is a relaxed, easy-going sort of place geared more towards local holidaymakers than to the international tourist trade. Families from Kuala Lumpur, Seremban and the surrounding region arrive in hordes during weekends and holidays to take advantage of the many modest hotels

PLATE 19   PAGES 74-75

and the good local food — and to patronise the itinerant ice-cream vendor on the beach. Snacks-on-wheels are as much a part of Malaysian life as hamburgers and hot dogs in the West, and small mobile foodstalls can be found everywhere.

Some of the four-wheelers boast quite elaborate "kitchens" serving *kway teow* or *laksa* (rich noodle-based dishes beloved by everyone). The two-wheelers' staple fare might be ice-cream, or *kacang* (nuts), or *krupuk* (large, feather-light prawn wafers) handed out from a huge bin of polished tin or brass strapped to the back of the bicycle.

I had quite a hard time setting up this shot. I wanted the "snacks-on-wheels" in sharp focus against a soft background, so depth-of-field was critical; I wanted the bicycle on the water's edge, but the tide was rising fast. Fiddle, twist, turn, adjust. Finally everything was ready, the ice-cream man patiently standing still. I pulled my head out from under the viewing hood, reached for the film holder, slid it in, looked up for a last check before removing the black slide and pressing the cable release — and he'd disappeared! He thought the shot was complete when I emerged from the hood. So, we started all over again. He was very cooperative, though I must have cost him quite a few dollars in business, for he'd been doing a very brisk trade.

The viewing screen is another tribulation for eight-by-tenners, for your subjects don't realise there's no film in the camera when you're shrouded under the black hood. My experience with the ice-cream man was typical.

At Port Dickson I turned inland to Seremban. A

PLATE 20　　　　　　PAGES 30-31

huge storm was building up, so I sped on for Kajang, renowned for the finest *satay* in Malaysia. A little before Kajang I was moved by the graphic quality of a land development project — a line of old rubber trees crowning a sheer wall of pink and red laterite, an increasingly common sight as more land is cleared for new housing estates.

The heavens opened before I got to Kajang, and the rain was drenching. I sought shelter at a very large *kampung* house. There was a plastic awning stretched out across the yard, and I gratefully wheeled the BMW underneath — to be confronted by an array of huge cooking pots filled with rice and delicious curries. Almost before I knew what was happening, I had been refreshed with glasses of rosewater and replenished with copious plates of chicken, fish, rice and all the trimmings. I should by now be accustomed to such open-hearted hospitality; nevertheless, it's a strange feeling to be treated as the guest of honour at a wedding to which you haven't been invited!

Inside the house, the main room had been prepared for the *bersanding* that would take place on the following day. This ceremonial "sitting-in-state" occurs after the simple religious ritual of marriage, and is the time when the new husband and wife are honoured as king and queen for the day, seated on their thrones to receive tribute and best wishes from family, relatives and friends. The newlyweds are supposed to remain impassive and unsmiling, even when teased with subtle innuendo and knowing smiles. (I've been asked why the "thrones" are empty in this shot. Two reasons: first, there's a sense of anticipation, of something to come; second, it's a chance to put yourself into *their* seats, to imagine how *you* would keep a straight face — especially when your guests are more occupied with eating wonderful food and talking to one another above the strident sound of electric guitars at full blast.)

My request to photograph the room had been granted. Outside, the rain continued to pour down; inside, there were forty people — no great problem, except the wooden house was raised on stilts, and shud-

PLATE 21　　　　　PAGE 40

dered every time anyone moved. I framed the shot, took a meter reading of four minutes, and somehow managed to get everyone to stay still. Not a muscle moved. Open shutter. Three minutes into the shot, a commotion outside: the bridegroom's entourage had arrived from Alor Setar. Frantic whisperings and hand signals. Nobody budged. Thirty seconds to go. Twenty, ten, *habis*! Finished! The room rocked as half-drowned guests escaped the rain. And there wasn't a single murmur of complaint.

Bypassing KL this time, my route took me across country from Kajang to Kelang along a narrow, winding, beautiful road. It was still raining. I decided to push on to Kuala Selangor, which I reached about six

PLATE 22　　　　　PAGES 82-83

o'clock in the evening. The rain had stopped, and clouds were sitting on top of the fading sunlight. By the time I found this estuarine village, the sunset was over, the sky suffused with its afterglow. I took a twelve-second exposure at a very small aperture, left the camera and tripod locked in position until the night was totally dark, then exposed the same sheet of film to burn in the village lights.

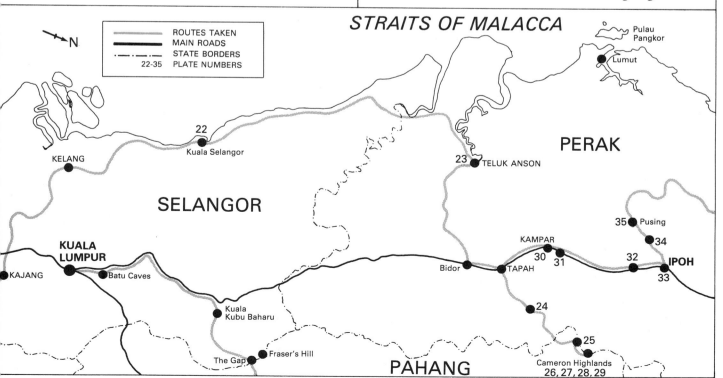

PLATE 23   PAGES 130-131

Few people visit Kuala Selangor; fewer still venture farther north along the coast and then inland to Teluk Anson. A pity, because it's an interesting, leisurely drive through immense oil palm estates and occasional stretches of flat, swampy land filled with birdlife. Teluk Anson's "leaning tower" is the chief attraction of an otherwise quite town. I left Teluk Anson in the early afternoon, aiming to get to the Cameron Highlands that evening. It was not a difficult journey, being just a hundred kilometres on good roads, with plenty of photographic distractions along the way. The road I took from Teluk Anson rejoins the main northern road at Bidor, only thirteen kilometres from Tapah and the turn-off to the highlands. Although the road skirts the central range, it nudges the foothills and begins to offer views quite different from those of the alluvial plains. Here you can start to sense the presence of the jungle, of vegetation quite ready to engulf the trails hacked out by man and his machines. Beyond Tapah the road climbs more steeply; the air is cooler, and the fragile tracery of tree

PLATE 24   PAGE 143

PLATE 25   PAGE 146

ferns fills your vision. These beautiful ferns are a poem of elegance and symmetry — but to find one that is perfect (without nicks and notches in its delicate sprays) can take hours. You see perfection, but you cannot get close enough to it for the ultimate shot, for the stunner that freezes this skeletal umbrella like a fly in amber. There's a precipitous drop between you and the foot of the tree; there's nowhere to brace your tripod's legs in the soft, leafy mulch; or the ground is firm, and the light is wrong.

At long last, Cameron Highlands. It's easy to understand why the colonial British took frequent refuge here from the heat and humidity of the sultry plains; why Malaysians flock here today whenever there's a long weekend or a holiday to give them time off from pressing city tasks. At more than fifteen hundred metres above sea level, this is the place for winter woollies and log fires (even though you're precisely 4° 30′ north of the equator); you'll never freeze, but the

PLATE 26   PAGE 161

cold can be intimidating if you're not prepared. "The Camerons" embrace a large area of land, much more than a single high peak thrusting through the mist. In the high-country valleys, on the small plateaux between ridges, gardens of astonishing richness produce their blooms or vegetables.

This blaze of colour was a very difficult shot, needing almost total

PLATE 27   PAGE 160

"tilt" in order to achieve full depth of field from the flowers in the front to those in the back; it took an hour to set up, and the camera was just centimetres from an overhead canopy of plastic that shielded the flowers from heavy storms.

"Kids among the cabbages" should have been a little easier (though the depth-of-field problems were similar), but it took a task force of parents, aunties and elder cousins to convince the children that the camera wouldn't eat them.

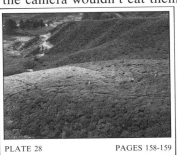

PLATE 28   PAGES 158-159

Flowers, vegetables, and tea. Hectare upon hectare of tea bushes, flowing over the highland slopes. This shot was taken in the early morning at the Blue Valley estate, on the way up to Gunung Batu Berinchang — at just on two thousand metres, the highest point in Malaysia accessible by road. From a distance, the soft folds of the estates look like patted-down wads of cottonwool; close up, they're tight knots of scratching, tearing bushes.

The Camerons, in their gentle guise, are a vast upland market garden growing lettuces and roses for the delectation of hot lowlanders. But from certain

PLATE 29   PAGES 164-165

vantage points the awesome spread of the rain forest and jungle makes you realise that much of Malaysia is still untamed, still largely unexplored; the fact that the mountain terrain is difficult to clear and cultivate is pretty much irrelevant — what hits you between the eyes is just how much of the country is wild and untouched. This view, from just below the summit of Gunung Batu Berinchang, is typical of those along the peninsula's spine.

On to Ipoh. Twenty kilometres from Tapah is Kampar, which I chose to represent the "typical" medium-sized Malaysian town. Medium? Well, according to statistical records, with a population between ten and fifty thousand. Kampar is somewhere at the lower end of that scale, and in a way is comparable to a mid-Western "middle America" town in the USA — except

PLATE 30   PAGES 126-127

that Malaysian towns must be *felt*, not compared! Where else can you find neat lines of shop-houses (old or new doesn't matter) in which a bicycle-repair business shares premises with a one-man tailoring establishment (*tukang jahit*); where the ubiquitous smallgoods store (*kedai runcit*) sells everything from cast-iron cooking pots to the finest silken threads? Every town has its distinctive character, yet there's common ground in the ferment of activity enlivening them all.

Close to Kampar, and easily seen from the road, is a handsome Chinese cemetery. I clambered up a hillock

PLATE 31   PAGES 54-55

for a better view, and chance once again intervened, this time in the form of an Indian cow-man coaxing his herd to other pastures. Cemeteries like this are invariably sited on hills. During the annual festival of Ch'ing Ming, the tombs are cleaned and the ground around them is cleared of grass and weeds. On the day of the festival itself, which normally falls in early April, offerings of food, fruit and wine are made to ancestors, and incense is burnt at their graves. Ch'ing Ming (also known as All Souls' Day) is an important date in the Chinese religious calendar.

Between Kampar and Ipoh the landscape is scarred with the remains of disused tin mines and spotted with

PLATE 32   PAGES 26-27

sheer outcrops of limestone, many of which contain caves. Some of the caves at or close to ground level are used as shrines by the Chinese and by Hindu Indians.

I found this billboard near Sam Poh Tong, the largest of the cavern temples, about six kilometres from Ipoh. It struck me as a wry comment on a landscape so manipulated by man.

Ipoh, the capital of Perak, owes its existence and success to the vast lodes of alluvial tin ore found in the

PLATE 33   PAGE 97

region. It is a large, prosperous town, though rather undistinguished from the visitor's point of view. One sight definitely worth seeing, however, is the dining-room of the venerable Station Hotel.

The "Station" was *the* hotel to stay in during colonial times, and even now it's easy to picture the *mems* and *tuans* sipping tea or a stengah (half-nip of whisky) in the Palladian grandeur of the dining hall. It is still an important centre for social contact in Ipoh.

I took this shot at about eleven in the morning. The day was black and thundery, so I asked for all the lights to be turned on — but even then I needed an exposure of eight minutes. A few people walked through the room while the shutter was open, but at such a long exposure they are visible only as a slight blur.

The western part of Perak, from Ipoh over to Lumut on the coast, is almost one vast open-cut tin mine. I

PLATE 34   PAGES 34-35

back-tracked slightly, going southwest to the old Chinese mining town of Pusing, and found this leviathan on the way. These huge mining dredges do everything but smelt the ore they collect. If you want a close-up view of such a dredge, approach it with caution — the soft, sandy edges of mining pools are liable to slip into the water at any

PLATE 35   PAGE 33

moment, and take you with them. Much safer to view are the traditional Chinese mine operations, like this one a kilometre or so from Pusing. On an even smaller scale, you can still see *dulang* washers at work in some places, hand-panning the tailings of the large mines for ore that has been missed.

The Dindings (between Pusing and the sea) is one of the oldest areas of tin mining and Chinese settlement in the peninsula; there are still a couple of tiny walled villages to be seen. And it was on the island of Pangkor, just off Lumut, that a treaty was signed between the British and local Malay rulers in 1874 — a step that heralded "intervention" and eventual British control over the federated and unfederated states. Until this time the British had merely been concerned with maintaining peace so that trade could prosper; despite minor skirmishes in Perak and inland from Melaka, they were reluctant colonialists.

There were mountains to the east and west as I rolled north to Kuala Kangsar on a really beautiful back-country road lined by huge old trees. It was a trip

PLATE 36   PAGES 134-135

that justified my love for the open road — and at the end of it was the promise of Kuala Kangsar.

It is a charming town on many counts, but its glory (without any doubt) is the magnificent Ubudiah Mosque, probably the finest example of traditional Muslim architecture in the country, with its huge onion-shaped dome pinned between four towering minarets.

Every major town has a "coffee-shop corner"; some, in fact, have several. This corner, in Kuala Kangsar,

PLATE 37   PAGES 92-93

seemed to me to sum up the allure and slightly raffish charm of such landmarks. It's got everything: the weddingcake architecture, the *makan* (food) cart, the brash clashes of colour.

Kuala Kangsar is also the royal capital of

PLATE 38   PAGES 132-133

Perak, and there are some fine examples of traditional Malay design in or near the town.

At the top of the list is this building (part of the *istana* or palace complex) with its marvellous gingerbread fretwork and sinuous ornament. In a world of plastic and stainless steel, it's like a kiss-of-life to find places created with such love and craftsmanship. For centuries, wood has been used in Malaysia for building and as a material to be carved into exquisite objects. Unhappily, wood perishes faster than brick, stone or tilework, and little remains of the woodcarver's art outside of regional museums.

The route from Kuala Kangsar to Maxwell Hill took me to the very pretty town of Taiping, famous for having the most beautiful and imaginatively planned Lake Gardens in the country—the lakes are old tin-mining pools, their shores now clothed with sweeping

PLATE 39   PAGES 156-157

lawns and lush tropical plants. Taiping's other attraction is Maxwell Hill, the oldest hill station on the peninsula. It has fewer facilities than the larger resorts like Cameron Highlands and Fraser's Hill, but its serenity is unrivalled. This Indian woman helps care for the garden of the Sultan of Perak's guest house. Prior to World War II, there was no road to Maxwell Hill, and visitors could make the twelve-kilometre journey on foot, on horseback, or in a sedan chair carried by bearers! The present road, completed in 1948, is only one lane wide and is barred to

private automobiles; you can get to the thousand-metre heights of Maxwell Hill by government Landrover from Taiping. I gratefully accepted the service on the way up, but coming down the following day I decided to walk part of the way. I bought my ticket, left my personal gear for a later Landrover to bring down, slung the tripod and camera over my shoulder, and set off. The air was refreshingly cool, the mountain

PLATE 40   PAGE 145

scenery inspiring. And I found this tree. Not perhaps remarkable as jungle trees go, except that it's rarely you can see one isolated like this—they're normally so hemmed in by relatives that you glimpse a huge trunk and nothing more, everything else being lost in a mass of foliage. Sometime later, the scheduled Landrover trundled down the hill and I hopped aboard.

Recalling that stroll, I sometimes wish I'd let the Landrover pass me by. Solitary walks along deserted jungle roads are to be treasured, not thrown away.

I was now less than a hundred kilometres from Butterworth and the vehicular ferry to Pulau Pinang, but I was anxious to re-visit some lesser known territory. I

PLATE 41   PAGES 16-17

rode back toward Kuala Kangsar, then swung north on the long, scenically fascinating road to Gerik. The land at first is quite flat, and ideal for growing rice. Farther on, the waters of the Perak River have swelled to form the calm spread of Tasek Chenderoh, a magical lake teeming with freshwater fish (dozens of fishermen with nets and fishing traps are proof of its largesse) and hemmed in by jungle-clad hills.

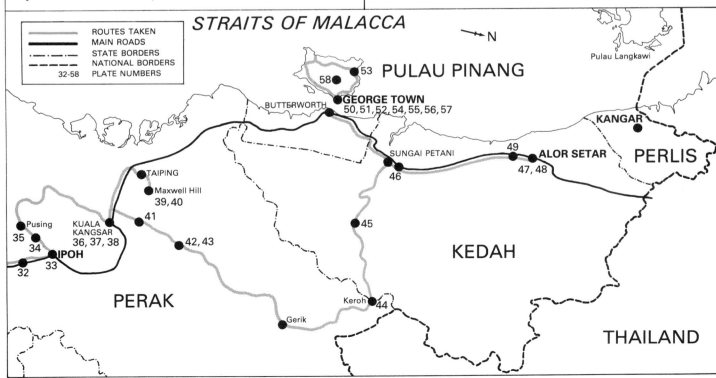

STRAITS OF MALACCA

→N

	ROUTES TAKEN
	MAIN ROADS
	STATE BORDERS
	NATIONAL BORDERS
32-58	PLATE NUMBERS

Pulau Langkawi

53 PULAU PINANG

58

BUTTERWORTH   GEORGE TOWN
50, 51, 52, 54, 55, 56, 57

KANGAR

SUNGAI PETANI   49   ALOR SETAR   PERLIS

46   47, 48

TAIPING

Maxwell Hill
39, 40

41

45

KEDAH

Pusing

35

34   KUALA KANGSAR
36, 37, 38   42, 43

32   33   IPOH

PERAK

Keroh 44

Gerik

THAILAND

PLATE 42   PAGE 50

PLATE 43   PAGE 37

Late that afternoon, just north of Tasek Chenderoh, I chanced upon this small village mosque. A far cry, perhaps, from the gilded glory of the Ubudiah Mosque, but still with a vital role to play in a rural community. By the time I got there, evening prayers were over and only a handful of worshippers remained, sitting outside the prayer hall to exchange views about the weather, the likelihood of a good rice harvest . . . .

Could I take a photograph? The answer, as usual, was "*boleh*", which literally translates as "can" (that is, "OK"), while embracing a number of subtle distinctions and variations—a very useful word in Malaysia. In any case, this out-of-the-blue arrival of the *orang gila* ("crazy man") with his monstrous bike and camera would be something to talk about for days. One of the appealing things about small Malaysian towns is just that: people work hard, but they also know how to relax without becoming bored with themselves or with one another.

Onward, ever onward. Through Gerik (the starting point for a new road to the east coast that will open to traffic in 1982 and revolutionise communications in the

PLATE 44   PAGES 128-129

far north), pushing up into the hills, then swinging a little to the northwest and the town of Keroh, with its wooden buildings and slightly Wild West atmosphere; I wouldn't be at all surprised to meet the shade of John Wayne or Gregory Peck (perhaps in some Asian manifestation) along the main street of towns like Gerik or Keroh—if you want to film the *bersilat* (Malay unarmed combat) version of *High Noon*, these are possible locations.

Not many foreign travellers get into these parts, though the long parabola north from Kuala Kangsar and back down to Pulau Pinang is one of the more interesting and exciting of Peninsula Malaysia's road routes.

At Keroh I linked up with the road running west

PLATE 45   PAGE 144

toward Sungai Petani. It is a winding route through some very lonely, lovely country, and almost eerie at times—nobody and nothing else but the omnipresent jungle.

About halfway to Sungai Petani I ran into a brief monsoon deluge accompanied by strong winds. I was forced to pull up, only to be rewarded (wet as I was) with this marvellous example of nature gone crazy: one tree growing on top of another, its roots gaining sustenance from the leaf-mould and the dead vegetation caught in the strong limbs of its foster parent.

PLATE 46   PAGES 2-3

Along the highway to the north of Sungai Petani are dozens of handsome old rubber estates. Ever since leaving Johor Bahru I had been looking for this kind of shot, where the trees touch above the road to form a long natural arcade. There were many times when I thought I'd found it, only to realise that my eyes had been playing tricks with me—the trees didn't really meet, or there were irregular patches where some did and some didn't, or a sharp bend in the road destroyed the corridor effect.

There was a lot of traffic, and I had to wait quite a time before opening the shutter for the exposure of one-eighth of a second; at that slow speed it was essential to have any vehicles as far away as possible so the blur of their movement would not be a distraction.

Farther north the land flattens out almost totally. This is an important rice-growing region, and the road follows an almost straight line through great expanses of *padi* before reaching Alor Setar, the capital of Kedah.

PLATE 47   PAGE 138

It is an attractive town, its centrepiece being the spacious *padang* (square) bordered by an interesting array of buildings. The superb Zahir Mosque was being renovated when I was there, so I decided to explore the Balai Besar (Great Hall) once used by the Sultan of Kedah on ceremonial occasions. I found this imposing gatehouse behind the hall, and was setting up the camera when the vendor-on-wheels came by. He stopped, curious to see what I was doing, and was perfectly happy to add a human dimension to what would otherwise have been a static "object" shot. Once again luck was with me.

For its size, Alor Setar is over-endowed with traffic roundabouts and one-way streets; moving around town becomes an exercise in making circles when all you

PLATE 48   PAGES 118-119

want is a straight line. Still, there was a happy result. Having to ride in circles, I passed this excellent example of the signpainter's art a couple of times on a Sunday. Monday, I went back to photograph it—and it had vanished, for the folding metal door had (of course) been closed back so the shop could open for business. The owner wasn't in, but I was able to persuade his young son to shut the screen just long enough for me to take the shot. The graphics of the painted pedestrian crossing were simply a bonus.

(A point about "graphics". If they're to be the sole theme of your photo essay, fine; if you also want a sense of time and place to register, then try to include a human touch. The Melaka stairway tiles [PLATES 4 & 16] are "graphics", but within a context.)

189

PLATE 49   PAGE 51

Most travelling salesmen want a tour of duty in northern Kedah or Perlis (the smallest state in Malaysia) because of the proximity of Haadyai, just over a hundred kilometres from Alor Setar across the Thai border, and renowned for its freewheeling nightlife.

I'm not a travelling salesman. I was retracing my steps, on the way back south toward Butterworth and Pulau Pinang, when I found this delightful small mosque, a perfect pairing to complement the one I had photographed a few days earlier near Tasek Chenderoh.

Pulau Pinang, the "island of the betel-nut tree", has sometimes been called the "pearl of the Orient"—perhaps a somewhat lavish epithet, but one that seems to me perfectly justified. It is not surprising that so many visitors to Malaysia make a special point of going to the island, for Pinang is really a microcosm of the peninsula: in George Town, it has an attractive, thriving, historically interesting capital city; it has high, jungle-clad peaks and secluded waterfalls; its beaches, fringed by casuarinas and coconut palms, come close to being everyone's dream of a "tropic paradise"; and there are also plenty of quiet corners where the relaxed lifestyle of the rural *kampung* or the fishing village can be experienced.

Pinang in 1786 was a sparsely populated island in the domain of the Sultan of Kedah. The Dutch controlled trading ports on both sides of the Straits of Malacca, including old Melaka (which had lost most of its former power with the growth of Dutch Batavia—modern Jakarta—on the north coast of Java). The Sultan was continually worried by the possibility of Siamese or Burmese incursions into his territory, while the British were anxious to find a foothold where they could safely shelter and replenish their trading vessels working between Bombay and China.

Captain Francis Light, an English trading master, was on good terms with the Sultan, and had access to important ears in the East India Company's Bengal headquarters. Light recommended the island as a provisioning and trading base; the Sultan agreed to cede Pinang; the Company reluctantly endorsed the move; and on 11 August 1786, on the north coast, Light hoisted the Union Jack and bestowed the name Prince of Wales Island on the new possession.

The formal treaty of cession between the Sultan and the Company was not signed until 1791, but by then Penang (as it was known for the next one hundred and sixty years) was rapidly becoming a prize jewel in the East India Company's crown of territories. It had a population of some twenty-five thousand by 1794, the year that Light died (his handsome tomb can be seen in the old Christian cemetery on Farquhar Street), and between 1826 and 1830 it was the capital of the "Straits Settlements" comprising Pulau Pinang, Melaka and Singapore.

Kedah had long been important as a source of tin, and glistening ingots remain a familiar sight on the wharves of George Town. Rubber, in later years, became another important export commodity. And what about betel-nut, which gave the island its original name? Strictly speaking, there's no such thing. I know that sounds like a heresy, but the so-called "betel-nut" chewed by many Indians and Malays, and by older women in particular, is actually a quid or wad (*sirih* or *sireh*) consisting of the nut of the areca palm—also the "Pinang" palm—smeared with a dob of lime paste and sometimes a touch of gambier, and all wrapped up in the peppery leaf of the betel plant (which is *not* a palm). Confused? So is everybody else, because nowadays areca palm and betel-nut palm are regarded as synonymous. Whatever the linguistic purists might say, if you enjoy *sirih* you are enjoying betel-nut, and that's that!

Pinang, like Singapore (founded as a British trading post thirty-three years later), was the goal of many

PLATE 50   PAGES 106-107

emigrants from the southern provinces of China. Most of those arriving in Pinang were from Fukien, and spoke Hokkien. Over the years they erected some of the biggest and most striking temples and clan houses to be seen in Malaysia, and their celebration of traditional Chinese festivals remains one of the more colourful aspects of Pinang's life, as these huge incense sticks clearly show. Another long-established feature of Chinese culture is the puppet-theatre. Movies, television and new-fangled devices like VTR have killed off many of the old travelling

PLATE 51   PAGES 116-117

troupes of puppeteers, but some survive and make occasional appearances at temple festivals. This troupe had ventured across the border from southern Thailand. I had watched a performance the day before this shot was taken, but would have had to stop the show (which was very well attended) in order to photograph it. I went back the next morning, and the puppeteers were pleased to do this "set-up" for me. It's not a "live performance", but the feeling of the real thing comes across.

Hand-painted cinema posters are a superb, though sadly neglected, art form in Malaysia, and the talent

PLATE 52   PAGE 139

that goes into their creation also expresses itself in other examples of the signpainter's skill. I found this billboard in a back street of George Town, and was immediately impressed by its true-to-life yet slightly surrealistic quality—and by the contrast of a thoroughly modern miss dominating the wall of a thoroughly old shop-house.

Another side to Pinang is the seemingly changeless lifestyle of the fishing villages along the northern and western coasts. I left George Town on an anticlockwise circuit of the island, passing through the beach resort area of Batu Feringgi (Portuguese Rock) with its amalgam of deluxe international hotels and

PLATE 53　　　　　　PAGES 64-65

subdued old-fashioned guest houses. At Teluk Bahang, where the road swings south, there's a rather muddy sandbank where the fishermen moor their boats at high tide; at low tide the boats are stranded, with time enough to scrape down a hull or seal a leak with caulking pitch. In the early morning, with the aroma of freshly brewed local coffee mingling with honest sea smells, this is an enchanting haven. And the food, in the small *kedai makan* (food shops) along this coast, is mouthwatering.

To those of you unfamiliar with Malaysia, I probably seem to be spending an exorbitant amount of time extolling the country's culinary virtues. I confess that I love the local food, whether it be Malay, Chinese or Indian. I should also add that it is impossible to stay here for more than a week or so without becoming aware of the passion with which Malaysians recommend (or defend) a favourite eatery: everybody seems to know *the* place for the finest steamed fish, noodles with spicy sauce, chicken rice, *satay*, chilli crab, savoury pancakes, rice porridge, prawn curry, steamed buns, smoked honey pork . . .

Not that "everybody" agrees on the finest, but if a favourite hawker moves his stand from Jalan Abu Bakar to Jalan Loke Yew or a new multi-storey food-hawkers' site, you can bet your next week of breakfasts that the local gourmands will know.

Of the many Chinese clan houses in Malaysia, none is more beautiful, more famous or more richly endowed

PLATE 54　　　　　PAGES 114-115

than that of the Khoo clan in Pinang, where there have been Khoos since before the arrival of Francis Light. In Cannon Square, at the end of Pitt Street, this magnificent clan-house (the celebrated Khoo Kongsi, or "hall of the Khoo group") has stood since 1906; the first *kongsi*, built in 1894, was destroyed by fire on the eve of Chinese New Year in 1901. In the central and largest of the *kongsi*'s three halls is this altar dedicated to Tau

PLATE 55　　　　PAGE 113

Sai Yeah, surrounded by intricate gilded carvings and paintings of legendary heroes and heroines. On the other side of the stone-flagged square, facing the *kongsi*, is a permanent stage for the performance of Chinese opera. Clan associations are rather like mutual benefit societies on a family-related basis, with wealthier members assisting the poorer in matters of health, education and (if need be) a daily living allowance.

Heading west across the top of the island, along

PLATE 56　　　　　PAGE 103

PLATE 57　　　　　PAGE 102

Northam Road toward the glittering beaches of Batu Feringgi, you'll find several examples of houses built in the early years of this century by wealthy mining magnates and business entrepreneurs. Every one of these pastel-tinted creations sits isolated in the midst of a vast expanse of close-cropped lawn. You can almost hear the clip-clop of horses drawing a brougham or a victoria, or the brassy beep of a horn announcing the arrival of a high-chassis deDion-Bouton as illustrious visitors call for an indubitably English tea at five in the afternoon. Houses like these are not old enough to be classified as "historic monuments", but it's to be hoped that they survive, along with many of Pinang's early architectural gems, as reminders of the island's often elegant past.

Finally, if there must be "finally" on an island with so many pleasant diversions to offer, there is Bukit Pinang (Pinang Hill), where the air is cool and from the top of

PLATE 58　　　　　PAGES 140-141

which the views are quite stunning. The funicular railway line to the top of The Hill was opened in 1923, and has operated ever since (though new carriages were put into service a couple of years ago). I took this shot of George Town and its suburbs shortly after sunset on a thirty-minute exposure. There should perhaps be more photographs of Pulau Pinang in this book—but beautiful as it is, it's only a tiny portion of what Malaysia has to offer.

"And, as the sun sinks in the west, we say a regretful farewell to this isle of dreams . . ." I always wanted the old James Fitzpatrick Travelogues to mention the sun setting in the east, but they never did (though Hollywood exceeded all my expectations, about ten years ago, with a film called *Krakatoa: East of Java* — that infamous volcanic island sits at the western end of Java, but I guess "east" sounded more exotic and mysterious).

The west coast of Peninsular Malaysia, through Melaka to Perlis and back to Pulau Pinang, has a great deal to interest the traveller with only a little time to spare: you can take a quick round-trip from Singapore to Melaka; a similar jaunt from KL to Melaka; a fast drive from KL through Ipoh to Pinang; a leisurely circuit from Pinang inland through Taiping and Gerik to Keroh and Sungai Petani; or, farther north, to Alor Setar and the boat service across to the serenely lovely Langkawi Islands. Nor should a day or so at one of the cool, upland resorts (the "hill stations" beloved by the British—Camerons Highlands, Maxwell Hill) be overlooked.

But there is, emphatically, the east coast. In many ways, a different world: more conservative, more traditional in its observances, and more happily blessed with some of the most glorious beaches and pyrotechnically brilliant coral reefs in the world.

At first sight, this claim might seem extravagant—but follow me. My second route started in Johor Bahru, capital city of the state of Johor and just across the road-and-rail causeway linking the southern tip of the peninsula with Singapore. (Johor Lama, or "Old Johor", lying inland from modern JB, is now only a small *kampung*, but there are remains of defensive earthworks that protected it when it was the original Johor capital. Founded about 1540 by a son of the last Malacca Sultan, it was sacked by the Portuguese in 1587.)

PLATE 59   PAGE 32

The suburbs of the city of JB straggle out into the countryside, where land development projects bear names like *Taman Emas* ("golden garden") and new housing estates seem to sprout overnight like mushrooms. I waited for some time at such a site for these tractors to converge. Then it was on through Kota Tinggi (with a lovely but over-populated waterfall nearby and endless groves of oil palm and rubber trees to the fishing town of Mersing. The BMW and I

PLATE 60   PAGES 60-61

seem to attract rain. This time, luckily, the rain had left Mersing before I reached it, though these fishing boats were still shining wet and gleaming in the light of early evening. The town is also the main departure point for boat trips to the nearby islands of Pulau Tioman (where many of the location scenes for the film version of *South Pacific* were shot), Pulau Rawa (with comfortable thatched "chalets" for rent on the edge of a beach and coral lagoon), the Hujong group and, slightly farther afield, the islands of Aur and Pemangill, much favoured by SCUBA-divers, coral-lovers and conchologists. The waters of the South China Sea, which surround these exquisite and easily accessible islands, are calm and clear for most of the year, except during and immediately after the northeast monsoon (November to early February).

Many islanders earn a living from fishing or from harvesting rights on the coconut groves that smother

PLATE 61   PAGE 20

the islands' foreshores and ramble inland to the foothills. I met this young Malay in one such grove. Relaxed, friendly and goodlooking, he typifies the people in this area.

I don't have any shots of coral, because as far as I know nobody has perfected an underwater housing for an 8×10 camera — when they do, I'll have an ideal excuse to get back to these islands.

I stayed for two days with the *penghulu* (headman)

PLATE 62   PAGES 48-49

of one of the island villages. He was charming, gentle, strong-willed, and altogether at peace with himself and the world; an inherently good man. I have roamed these islands, have basked in the sun waiting for the next ripe coconut to fall, have dived with a sharp stick to harpoon stingrays (freshly caught, smoked over a fire of coconut husk, a real piscine delicacy) . . . the islands, and the islanders, are among my great loves.

Back on the mainland I stayed a night at the govern-

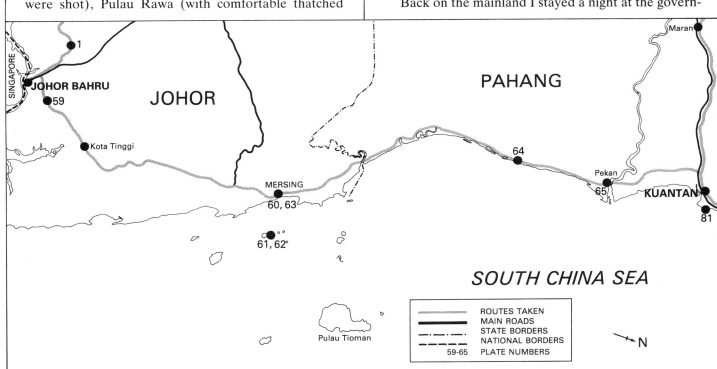

ment rest house in Mersing, with its distant view of the

PLATE 63 PAGE 147

"ass's ears" (two high peaks on Tioman, for centuries a mariner's landmark). From the balcony of the rest house I had this straight-on view into the heart of a "Traveller's Palm", whose delicate fan-like stems and leaves have always intrigued visitors to Malaysia. "Are the branches specially clipped?" they always ask. The answer is no; it's probably the only two-dimensional tree in the world.

Beyond Mersing the jungly and sometimes marshy terrain to the west is counterpointed by enticingly long stretches of utterly deserted sand and gentle aquamarine waves, which change their colour and mood within minutes as storm clouds build up on the horizon. Most people avoid the east coast at the onset of the

PLATE 64 PAGE 57

northeast monsoon (about the beginning of November), but I have always loved the purple-black skies and whipped-cream wave tops of that awesome season. The light, too, is constantly changing, creating a dramatic *son et lumière* accompanied by the roll of thunder.

The journey north was once punctuated by delays at rivers where ferries were the only means of crossing. Now all of the east coast rivers up to the Thai border are bridged, and so I enjoyed a pleasant ride to the royal town of Pekan, the residence of the Sultan of Pahang (who is currently Malaysia's Yang di-Pertuan Agung, or King). Pekan is an attractive place, with an interesting museum containing mementoes of the Pahang Sultans, and two fine mosques.

PLATE 65 PAGE 94

I stopped off at a coffee shop for a bowl of *mee goreng*, and was delighted by its TV set and ornaments. The rest of the customers thought I must be mad, wanting to photograph it, and the whole place was soon rocking with goodnatured laughter.

From Pekan to Kuantan, the commercial centre and capital of Pahang, it's an easy drive of forty-four kilometres. Kuantan is the gateway to the most distinctive half of the east coast. Because most visitors come to it through Kuala Lumpur, I now move on to my third peninsular route, beginning at the national capital; the east coast journey continues with PLATE 81.

In 1857, a party of eighty-seven Chinese tin miners employed by Raja Jumaat (one of the six territorial chiefs of Selangor) was sent up-river from Kelang to search for ore deposits. At Ampang, a little beyond the junction of the Kelang and Gombak Rivers, they found an enormously rich lode — and within a month sixty-nine of them had died of malaria. But others followed, and this muddy river junction became a supply post, then a village, then a town wracked by violence and sudden death. Not that death was any stranger to those turbulent days, for as Sir Frank Swettenham wrote in *British Malaya*, only occasional periods of quiet inter-

rupted Selangor's normal state of "robbery, battle and murder". Local Malay chiefs, descendants of the piratical Bugis from Sulawesi (Celebes) who had founded Selangor in the eighteenth century, were constantly at war; while the Chinese miners, with everything to gain and nothing to lose, engaged in a continual series of *tong* battles.

Looking at Kuala Lumpur today, it is almost impossible to imagine the bloody tumult of one hundred

PLATE 66 PAGES 88-89

and twenty years ago. The infant settlement was burned to the ground on three occasions; yet, if ever a phoenix arose from the ashes, this is it!

KL's "Moorish-rococo" railway station (RIGHT), a very substantial relic of the British Empire's glorious years between 1900 and the outbreak of World War I, is still a favourite camera study for tourists. Five years ago, the aggressively modern skyline beyond its domes and minarets didn't even exist (in some parts of the city, yes, but not here); even so, the need to build ever upward is unlikely to affect Kuala Lumpur's colonial treasures, for the railway station, the monumental Secretariat Building facing the *padang*, and other odds and ends have become an essential part of the city's distinctive character.

I'm never sure whether I'm more impressed by the

PLATE 67 PAGE 91

station or by the building on the opposite side of the road housing the administrative offices of Keretapi Tanah Melayu (KTM, the Malayan Railway). On this occasion KTM won with its bold wood-and-paper diesel locomotive exhorting Malaysians to "discipline and loyalty", the theme of 1980's national celebration of independence, gained on 31 August

1957 when the sovereign Federation of Malaya (later Malaysia) came into being.

KL has seven hotels in the three- to five-star luxury class, and more are on the way. I've stayed in some, and they're good. But being a traveller with a penchant for the traditional or out-of-the-ordinary, I cannot disguise my attachment to Malaysia's older "establishments" where some of the waiters and room-boys have served faithfully for thirty or more years. The nostalgic Hotel Majestic, right next to the KTM building, is an example. It was built in 1932 to the design of a Dutch architect; the four-person "cage" elevator and the

PLATE 68 PAGE 96

phone booth are collector's items; and the father of the present manageress, Madam Lim Toan Lin, was managing director of the hotel from 1935 until 1970.

This shot was taken from the *top* of the covered walkway leading into the lobby. I guess I could see Hobbits creeping in beneath the "ENTRANCE" sign.

The swing-chair was in a corner

PLATE 69   PAGE 95

of the garden where delicious *satay* is served. For me, it summed up the sadly tatty grandeur of a past age.

Madam Lim, when she saw colour proofs of the shots some weeks later, was not amused. "People will think we don't look after the hotel." I tried to reassure her that all Westerners are a little bit mad, and *love* these fleeting contacts with a lifestyle they know only from reading Conrad or Maugham. She was mollified, but clearly unconvinced. On the other hand, the Majestic enjoys an average ninety-five percent occupancy rate, and from experience I know the occupants go there *because* it's in touch with a bygone era. Incidentally, the broken swing-chair had been repaired (and swings!) long before I had returned to KL with the colour proofs.

There's another side of KL that yanks you abruptly into the 1980s and makes it abundantly clear that here is a city set on commercial and financial growth as the capital of a nation rich in export commodities. "Down

PLATE 70   PAGE 90

town", within a radius of about a kilometre from the point where the Kelang and Gombak Rivers meet, banking and insurance companies have been erecting multi-storey office buildings by the dozen.

The podium block of Bank Bumiputra, on Jalan Melaka, is architecturally the most original of the new giants. Based on a traditional east coast wooden house (though on a much larger scale), it is completely clad in golden-brown Langkawi marble quarried on the island of the same name in the far northwest of the peninsula.

Not all of Langkawi's marble is this colour: some is pale green, some cream, some white. It has been extensively used in Malaysia's buildings, and nowhere more strikingly than in the capital.

Among the most impressive of KL's modern architectural masterpieces are the noble Parliament Building, set in hectares of green grass; and the boldly imaginative International Airport at Subang.

One of my minor travelling pleasures is a morning shave — not standing in front of a bathroom mirror, but

PLATE 71   PAGE 87

comfortably seated in a barber's chair while a wicked-looking cut-throat razor removes my whiskers in a flash of hot foam and cool steel.

Just to make sure you get the message, this establishment proclaims the nature of its business in four languages: Malay, English, Chinese and Tamil. The shot was difficult, for I was standing in the centre of Jalan Cheng Lock, one of the busiest streets in KL, and I had to wait nearly half an hour for a suitable break in the traffic. The barbers (one of whom had shaved me earlier) didn't seem to mind being called away from their customers three or four times; I don't know what their customers thought!

Needing to reload the film-holders, I sought out the nearest photographic studio; as usual, the proprietor

PLATE 72   PAGES 104-105

was willing to let me use his darkroom. While there I noticed this hand-coloured family portrait, taken about 1930.

The young boy fifth from the right is today the owner of the studio; before him, it had been run by his father; and before that, by his grandfather, who set up business as a photographer in Shanghai before the turn of the century and later migrated to Malaya.

PLATE 73   PAGE 136

I met this little Malay schoolgirl in the grounds of the magnificent Masjid Negara (the National Mosque), a brilliant example of modern Islamic architecture completed in 1965.

Her wimple-like headdress is in the style worn by many Muslim women in Malaysia, and is a "uniform" at schools like the one attached to the National Mosque. The sign behind her, in English and Bahasa Malaysia (the national language), politely requests visitors to dress decorously before entering the mosque.

The fastest overland route from KL to Kuantan runs east across the peninsula, past Bentong and through Temerloh. It is a good road, with some attractive mountain scenery; it is also a very busy road, and not to be recommended if you're interested in leisurely travel (of course, if you're in a hurry to reach the east coast, it's ideal).

My preference is the longer and much more beautiful route through The Gap and along some of the back roads of Pahang. The start is not especially propitious, for the first ten or so kilometres north of KL are famous for their traffic jams and vistas of tin-mining desolation.

PLATE 74   PAGE 154

Then suddenly, on the right, there looms the gigantic limestone outcrop containing the Batu Caves, among the outstanding natural sights on the peninsula. The caves, "discovered" in 1878 by an American naturalist, have become famous as a pilgrimage point for thousands of Hindus during the annual Thaipusam festival, when penitents bearing spiked harnesses (*kavadi*) carry their painful burden up the two hundred and seventy-two steps to the main cavern in honour of Lord Subramaniam, son of Shiva, to whom this shrine is dedicated.

Of the twenty caves, the most spectacular is the so-called "Cathedral Cave", with a ceiling more than a hundred metres above the floor.

For once, a lack of light was on my side. Outside,

PLATE 75   PAGE 155

heavy cloud had obliterated the sun, thus reducing the contrast between cave-light and daylight. With an exposure of eight minutes I was able to capture shadow details without burning out the daylight areas. Small groups of people were moving through the cave during the exposure, but did not register on the film because of the extremely slow shutter speed.

Another sixty kilometres up the road is the turn-off for Kuala Kubu Baharu and Fraser's Hill. The road north of Batu Caves has improved enormously in the last three years, and there are some lovely scenic stretches through Templer Park, but the bends and steep grades keep heavy trucks crawling in low gear, and the congestion at times is almost as frustrating as KL's during the peak hour — though improvements will soon ease these travails. On such occasions I'm grateful for a powerful, manoeuvrable bike; I'm enjoying a glass of *kopi susu* thirty minutes ahead of anyone else.

Which I did in KKB. Among English-speaking Malaysians, if a place name can be reduced to a set of initials, it is. So we live with KL (Kuala Lumpur), PJ (Petaling Jaya, KL's huge satellite town), JB (Johor Bahru), KKB (Kuala Kubu Baharu), KB (Kota Bahru) . . . and so it goes.

And what about all these variations on *baru*? That remains one of the complexities of modern Malay. The word means "new", and has been rendered in *rumi* (Romanised spelling) in four ways that I know of: *baru*, *baharu*, *bharu*, and *bahru*. As far back as 1972, Indonesia and Malaysia got together on a system known as *ejaan baru*, the "new spelling", which sought to standardise the Romanisation of the Malay language shared by the two countries (the system has been a linguistic success). One example: Malaysia's "ch" and Indonesia's "tj", with their respective origins in English and Dutch spelling, have become a jointly acceptable "c" — except where traditional place or family names are concerned.

In the spelling of place names throughout this book, including its maps, the usage of the TDC has been followed as it appears on the excellent TDC Road Map

produced in 1978. Kelang, Gerik, Keroh and Setar (as in Alor Setar) are the accepted new spellings of Klang, Grik, Kroh and Star — but if you pronounce the new spellings the way the old names look, and as they appear on many other maps, you'll have no trouble finding your way around.

Malay is a supremely poetical and metaphorical language, full of richness and colour: *mata hari*, "eye of the day", is the sun; *makan angin*, "eating the wind", is to take a stroll; while just the sound of *lumba-lumba* suggests the rolling motion of, yes, a porpoise.

There have been times, of course, when the language hasn't quite been able to keep up with science. It may be an apocryphal story, but I've heard tell that the original Malay word for helicopter was *kapal terbang dengan kipas atas*, a "flying boat with a fan on top". But times change, and I was once reprimanded for asking when the *keretapi* (literally, "carriage/fire", and hence train) would arrive. "Sir," said the Indian station master, "we are now having diesel locomotives. Using coal we are not. Please be speaking of the *teren*." So now I ask when the *teren* is going to leave or arrive, though I notice that Keretapi Tanah Melayu continues to flourish.

Some funny things have also happened; funny, I suppose, only to someone using English as a first language. Nevertheless, it's somewhat disconcerting to be barrelling along a highway and pass a large truck with the word *semen* emblazoned on its side, until you realise it's a cement lorry; it takes time to get accustomed to *fail* for file, *sains* for science; and I puzzled over *wok syop* and *fomen setor* for some time before I recognised our old British Railways friends "workshop" and "foreman's store" (what's wrong with *kedai kerja* for workshop? . . . a question that's sure to bring a thousand linguists down on my head like the proverbial ton of bricks).

After that brief detour into arcane matters, let's get back to the road. Once more I was heading toward the mountain range that is the high, bumpy spine of the

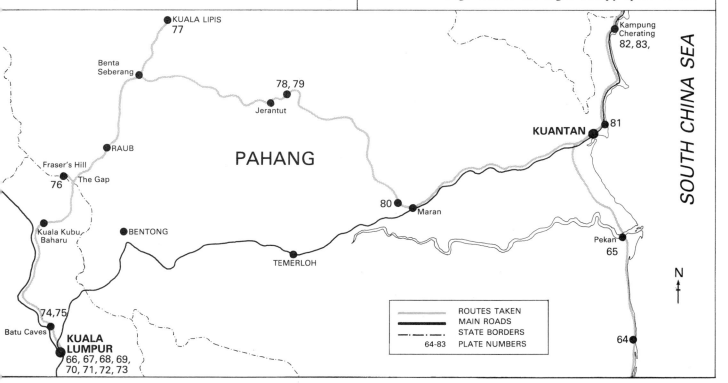

peninsula, and this time I was going over it. But first, a night's rest at The Gap, a high east-west pass across the mountains on the border of Selangor and Pahang.

The Gap Rest House looks like something out of an Emily Brontë novel. Standing on a bluff above the road, with its walls of greyish-blue granite and a trim garden of rose bushes and dahlias, it could have been transplanted from some remote corner of northern England. The wooden floors of the spacious, high-ceilinged rooms have a sheen you only ever see after decades of polishing; the brass window-locks gleam like special items in an antique shop; the rotating wooden bookcase in the sitting-room contains twenty-year-old copies of *British Industry*. I dined on steak, chips and peas, and after dinner relaxed in front of a generous log fire and talked with a thirty-ish Malay in the government service about . . . well, about everything.

At dawn, the whoop-whoop-whoop cry of gibbons snapped me back to reality. The reality saying Malaysia, not England. Six o'clock, and I was first through the gateway on the one-way labyrinthine road to Fraser's Hill, eight kilometres of mist-shrouded jungle, corkscrew corners and amazing beauty; the fresh, green smell of the highlands was almost as good as an early-morning cup of coffee.

I got to Fraser's, and the coffee had to wait. The light was soft and angular, the tiny nine-hole golf course was bathed in

PLATE 76　　　　PAGES 162-163

dew and shadow. I was back in Brontë country, complete with Wuthering Heights on the horizon.

Joggers in tracksuits were enjoying the crisp morning air; a party of Japanese golfers lined up for a photograph on the first tee; an Indian woman in a bright sari was meticulously sweeping the dew off the greens.

Fraser's is more compact than The Camerons, and more intimate in feeling. Bungalows of brick or stone hide away along small roads traversing tree-clad ridges and ferny gullies, and there are some fine hotels.

After a breakfast of ham, bacon, eggs and sausages, with plenty of coffee and toast-and-marmalade (amazing what that mountain air does for your appetite), I took off for The Gap and swung eastward into Pahang through what I consider to be some of the most beautiful country in the peninsula. The narrow, winding road is enclosed by proud stands of huge trees, monarchs of the jungle. Occasionally a dead forest giant is shrouded with lush parasitic growth, or crowned by a mass of elkhorns or birds'-nest ferns. There are corners where clear mountain streams tumble down rocky beds surrounded by trailing vines and clumps of wild orchids.

Leaving the mountains and foothills I passed through Raub, the scene of a minor gold rush in the last century, and now a quiet, small town with a wide main street and the usual assortment of busy-looking shop-houses. At Benta Seberang I took a twenty-six-kilometre diversion to Kuala Lipis, one of my favourite "frontier" towns not far from the border of the National Park. The railway line from Kota Bharu to Kuala

Lumpur passes through here, but for cars or bikes it's the end of the road. The commercial and administrative sections of the town sit on different hills: below the main street the land slips away toward the river and a

PLATE 77　　　　PAGES 122-123

jumble of "ladder streets" lined with *makan* stalls; it was here that I found this truck, a lively mobile advertisement typifying the do-it-yourself entrepreneurial spirit of Malaysia (I could easily devote a book to ads-on-wheels). In another area there's an immense hill-top edifice that looks more like an ancient Assyrian fortress than a block of government offices (which it is). And there's the rest house perched on a knoll: wide wooden verandahs, a bold colour scheme of green and yellow, the usual mixture of CSO (Central Supplies Office) furniture, and an ambience that puts it close to the top of my list of places to stay.

Next day it was back to Benta Seberang and on to Jerantut, where I could have taken a southerly route to Temerloh and the trunk road to Kuantan; instead, I stayed on the back road that eventually joins the highway at Maran, only fifty kilometres from Kuantan.

It was not a good road, but there were plenty of compensations for its pot-holed surface: very little traffic, some wonderful patches of high-timber forest, a mongoose darting across the road, a half-glimpsed wild boar crashing through the undergrowth; later, as more signs of settlement began to appear (this is sparsely populated country), wandering families of goats and cows were more of a road hazard than timber trucks.

Then the devastation. Man-made, and with a specific goal in mind — the utilisation of the rolling lowlands. In recent years, millions of dollars have been poured into schemes involving a combination of resettlement and the exploitation of potential national resources. One of the chief agents in this investment programme is FELDA, the Federal Land Development Authority, which has substantial interests in rubber and oil palm.

I wouldn't be surprised if first-time travellers in the peninsula thought that hedgehogs live here. They don't, but anyone used to the sight of dead hedgehogs along Europe's lanes and byways would think so — except that the "hedgehogs" are the spiky, prickly remains of clumps of oil palm nuts that have fallen off the back of a high-laden truck (some, squashed flat by cavalcades of rubber tyres, look like wigs put through a mangle).

PLATE 78　　　　PAGE 21

These trucks were waiting to disgorge their cargoes of oil palm nuts at a processing plant some five or six kilometres off the Jerantut-Maran road. I had been intrigued by a pall of smoke on the horizon, thinking it might be a vast burning-off in progress, only to find that it was a chimneystack at the plant. There was a guard at the entrance to the plant compound, and a flurry of telephone calls when I started

196

setting up the camera. I had a *laissez passer* letter from TDC, which quickly settled any qualms about my taking the shot. When I asked for truck-driving volunteers to pose, I was almost swamped; typically, the five heroes were mercilessly cat-called and cheered on by another twenty laughing compatriots.

PLATE 79   PAGES 28-29

Within two years, this devastated landscape will be covered with a film of greenery as young oil palms, planted by hand when only twenty to thirty centimetres high, begin to feel confident outside of their nursery environment, where they have lived in tubs of tin or black plastic until old enough for transplanting.

PLATE 80   PAGE 15

Just short of Maran, and the link-up with the trunk route to Kuantan, this pretty corner caught my eye as being typical of these back-country roads, where the narrow path of bitumen is hemmed in on all sides by a wall of riotous growth. Maintenance gangs, armed with grass-cutters and the razor-edged *parang* (the Malay machete) are constantly patrolling these roads to keep back the tangle of lushness that threatens to engulf anything and everything.

To comfort the faint-hearted, I must say that I have seen very few snakes in Malaysia. (I've met more cobras in the compound of my house in Singapore than I've ever seen in ten years of traipsing through the wilds of the peninsula or Borneo.) Disappointingly, I must also report that I've seen very few wild animals. Wild boar, yes; an occasional elephant (on the road between Kota Tinggi and Mersing, but never in the jungle); sometimes a small deer, though never the tiny *kancil* or mouse-deer, a hero of many Malay folk-tales; glimpses of gibbons and other simian relatives, including an intrepid trio who invaded my hotel room in KL some years ago; and I've never seen a tiger in the wild, though it's not so long ago that they were reputed to attack at least one rubber tapper every day.

In fact some of the largest beasts I've seen weren't beasts at all; they were insects. Dead, fortunately. There are three or four stalls in the Cameron Highlands, along with many others selling fresh fruit, vegetables and cut flowers, that specialise in bugs brought in by the jungle-dwelling Orang Asli. Among the dozens of species of kaleidoscopically coloured butterflies (available, ready-mounted, in most KL souvenir shops) I once saw a black rhinoceros-horn beetle measuring ten centimetres from top to toe. I have *never* met anyone like him in the forest.

(It's also interesting to note how the vegetation, heat and humidity can get to you in the nicest possible way. A friend of mine who had lived here for quite a number of years went back to London on leave. It was summer — and he nearly froze to death in 15°C temperatures. But there was a solution. He rushed down to Kew Gardens, found the tropical greenhouse with its palms, tree-ferns, 95% humidity and 32°C heat, and sat there for hours reading Somerset Maugham's *Malayan Stories*. The only thing missing was a gin & tonic!)

Kuantan, the capital of Pahang, is a sprawling, very attractive town; a commercial centre for logging and plantation activity; and the gateway to the northern half of the east coast. The town itself sits a few kilometres up-river from the sea, but the beachfront sets the pace for tourism developments now reaching farther and farther up the coast.

Fresh out of the backwoods, I felt like a country bumpkin seeing the "big smoke" for the first time: azure swimming pools, long-limbed girls in bikinis, dimly lit bars that wouldn't shame Miami or Malaga — *la dolce vita* in a tropic setting. I took two shots that later ended up among the

PLATE 81   PAGES 66-67

rejects, then strolled along the beach to find this. At first sight, just any old boat cast up on the sand of a South China Sea beach.

In fact, the bleached remains of a Vietnamese refugee boat. It reached this shore some time during 1978, with perhaps a hundred people aboard. The political implications of its origin and arrival didn't touch me; what did strike me was the vision of so many people on such a small boat — and the contrast it offered when I raised my eyes and saw in the background a sumptuously appointed international hotel.

There is no doubt that the coast between Kuantan and Kota Bharu is soon to become "The Strip". Private and government-backed organisations are opening up resort areas, building luxurious hotels and holiday havens — but with a sensitivity and awareness of local culture and design that manages to combine all-mod-cons with a feeling for the indigenous way of life. For many years the west coast of the peninsula has been uppermost in travellers' minds — KL, Melaka, Pinang. Now, air services and improved roads are beginning to make the east coast more easily accessible; there is better accommodation; and (as even the most biased west-coaster would have to admit) the beaches are sandier and the sea is clearer.

I zoomed north from Kuantan along an excellent road to Kampong Cherating and the off-road site of the recently opened Club Méditerranée (the first to be established in Asia). Within a few hundred metres

PLATE 82   PAGE 68

of the Club complex I came across a romantic rocky outcrop where the incoming tide swirled and swooshed in gentle green eddies.

The east coast beaches may sometimes roll for tens of kilometres in an unbroken line; at other places they erupt in ragged coves and corners where you can laze in the sun and dream of a hidden pirate hoard. Wholly a dream? This was no Spanish Main, ravaged by Captain Kidd or John Morgan; yet until comparatively recent times piracy was also employment for many shore-based people on the South China Sea. Perhaps there's a treasure in jade and porcelain and gold lying below your beach towel?

Probably not. Not that it matters. Who could ask for

PLATE 83   PAGES 58-59

a more dramatically coloured or brilliant jewel than the sky itself as the first clouds of the· northeast monsoon gather on the horizon? The light shimmers with gold and green, the clouds assume the hues of a new bruise, the translucent sea turns surly and dark.

Such an exhilirating time to walk alone on a deserted, wind-swept beach, to be aware of sea smells and the increasing roar of the ocean; a time for solitude, for thought and reflection. And if you can't stand all this self-imposed isolation, you can always scamper back to the bar for a stiff noggin of your favourite tipple.

You might also wonder how fishermen fare on this lovely coast. How do they face up to the storms, the sun, the often unpredictable changes of weather? To look at their boats (even if you're an experienced sailor), your reaction is likely to be: "Go to sea in *that*!" But they do, and have done for generations. Sure, today there are diesel engines and 50 HP outboards and inflatable life-rafts. There are also many smaller boats, without any of the appurtenances of twentieth-century "civilisation", and *they* still go out through the waves. I've been with the men who crew them, been out on their fragile craft. "Why?" I ask. "To eat," is always the reply. "And you don't worry?". "*Inshaallah* . . . it's in the hands of God."

North of Cherating and the Club Med I reached Chukai, a few kilometres across the Pahang-Trengganu border. It was late in the afternoon, around five o'clock, and the boats were coming back with their daily catch. Some of the fish were already mummified in a wrapping of crushed ice; others, still kicking, were swiftly heaved ashore in wicker baskets, weighed on a huge hook-scale, and packed into layers of ice in boxes that were soon on the backs of trucks heading non-stop

PLATE 84   PAGES 80-81

for markets in KL and Singapore. Day in, day out. And when all the fish have been sent to wherever they're going, there's time in the few remaining hours of daylight to check the nets, to mend holes in the mesh.

I stood on a sandbank, my feet soaking wet, to take this shot. There were several other fishermen on the boat as I was setting up; none of them minded when I indicated that I wanted just one man as my subject (once again, the cooperation I had come to expect when people see the Deardorff in all its enormity — with an Instamatic, I'd still be trying to organise the crowd, or I'd have been taking a very different kind of shot). There was a strong

tidal stream moving the boat on its mooring line, and depth of field was critical; I had to set up fast, and shoot fast — not easy when your subject can be out of focus with a shift of only a few centimetres.

About three or four kilometres from Kemasik, in open scrubby country, I turned right along a dirt road to rediscover a secluded cove I'd known on earlier journeys. It's only a couple of hundred metres off the

PLATE 85   PAGE 69

highway, and most people flash past it without even knowing what they're missing. There's no hotel, no bar, not even a travelling *makan* stall — and no people.

I found what I'd remembered. An expanse of truly golden sand studded with strange lumps of granite; trees with an almost perverse desire to live, clinging to precarious foot-holds; and behind the point from which this shot was taken, a tiny bay hedged in by a scramble of rock enclosing a warren of smugglers' caves. Smugglers? On this coast? I'm a romantic, and I'm also a sceptic. The caves are small, haunting, marvellously exciting — and you can only get into them at low tide. I cannot imagine any self-respecting smuggler or pirate (another version of the same tale) seeking refuge here with so many kilometres of deserted beach to choose from.

In some ways Trengganu's coast is strangely empty. It's not an emptiness devoid of people, for there are always small villages and isolated houses sprinkled along the main road north; far more than you see in the hills of Pahang. So what is it? A number of things: coconut groves with their goat-trimmed grass between the palms; the way so many of the thatched houses blend with the landscape; and more than anything else, the open feeling of *kampung* and land. There's not the enclosing presence of the jungle. This is a lean, spare coastal strip (though the state of Trengganu thrusts into a mountainous hinterland and the eastern border of Taman Negara), and at times the vegetation is surprisingly thin and dry — squat shrubs on sandy hillocks, dunes lightly swathed with uncertain grass, inland lagoons edged with reeds and the skeletons of spindly bushes.

I love it. For itself, and also for its contrast with the fecund green life of the interior. It is essentially a coastal state, and much of its life turns on the fortunes of its fishermen and the moods of the seasons.

And here, more than anywhere else in Peninsular Malaysia, traditional culture survives.

Here is where you can still see performances of *wayang kulit*, the ancient "shadow puppet theatre" that has entranced audiences for more than a thousand years with stories taken from the Hindu epic, the *Ramayana*. The shadow play, a forerunner of movies and TV (or, perhaps more accurately, modern audio-visual shows), employs a cast sometimes running into the sixties; a semi-translucent screen on which shadows thrown by the "cast" are projected; a source of light strong enough to create hard-edged shadows; and the *dalang*, the master of ceremonies who combines the roles of producer, director, conductor and ventriloquist. The "cast" consists of flat, two-dimensional leather puppets cut from stiffened buffalo hide, mounted on thin stems of wood or bamboo, and generally with jointed arms that can be manipulated by the *dalang*. The *dalang* sits behind and below his screen, with the light burning above him, while he brings forward his characters in a stunning series of adventures, romantic interludes, fierce battles and court intrigues — and in front of the screen, watching this shadowy fairytale world, so full of action and vitality, sits the audience, rapt in attention to the ageless story, delighted by the skill of the *dalang* as he speaks the roles for all of his dozens of characters, improvising with verve and often with gusty humour. Even if you don't speak a word of Malay, the performance is a memorable experience.

Unfortunately, *wayang kulit* shows are increasingly rare these days, victims of the transistor radio and the TV screen. You might be lucky enough to chance on one at a *kampung* celebration (a wedding, perhaps), though the best idea is to ask at tourist offices in Kuantan or Kuala Trengganu; they can arrange performances, given reasonable notice and the prospect of a large enough audience (this is one time when group travel is an advantage).

Trengganu and its northern neighbour, Kelantan, are also traditionally the sites for top-spinning and kite-flying. If these sound like pastimes for children, you'll have to think again. Great strength is needed to set a seven-kilogram top on its way — and the fact that these superbly hand-crafted "toys" can spin for more than an hour takes them into the realm of sport as art. Similarly with the kites, in all their spectacular shapes and colours; young boys *do* play with them, but it's their fathers who pilot the giants that soar hundreds of metres into the air (not surprisingly, the emblem of MAS, Malaysia's national airline, is a kite).

Once again, top-spinning and kite-flying don't take place every day of the week, and your chances of stumbling on such a spectacle are fairly limited; nevertheless, you can arrange for exhibitions of these skills through state tourism offices (though kite-flying,

naturally, is at the mercy of the weather conditions). And it's always worthwhile checking with your hotel receptionist — some of the major hotels along the coast have regular "cultural nights" featuring local dances, and they seem to be in close contact with what's happening culturally.

And so onward, in beautiful weather. Sunshine, glimpses of the South China Sea through coconut groves, an open road mercifully free of really heavy traffic. One pleasing thing about tourism development on this coast is the adoption of local styles and local building materials: Club Med, back at Cherating, is built largely of wood in a free (and successful) adaptation of traditional east coast architecture; so too is the TDC's recently opened luxury hotel at Tanjung Jara, just north of Kuala Dungun; and the same goes for the small, beautifully sited Rantau Abang Visitors Centre.

Rantau Abang has a unique claim to fame: its turtles. Here, along a thirty-kilometre stretch of beach, giant leatherback turtles arrive from as far away as the Atlantic Ocean to lay their eggs between May and September each year (August being the peak month). How and why they return to this isolated spot remains one of nature's mysteries. But they do, crawling ashore at night to dig a hole with their hind flippers and deposit up to a hundred eggs. When the young turtles hatch, some fifty days later, they are prey to innumerable predators (birds, crabs — and man), but supervision by the Malaysian Department of Fisheries now ensures that at least forty thousand succeed in their struggle to reach the sea and maintain the cycle.

Then, Kuala Trengganu, with its fascinating market — under the branches of huge old trees, an incredible variety of goods laid out on packing cases, cardboard boxes and sheets of newspaper: fish of all sizes in a hundred subtle hues of silver, pink and green, a riot of ominous-looking (but delicious) vegetables, axe-heads and wickedly sharp *parang-parang* alongside a display of patent medicines and tubes of "Darkie" toothpaste.

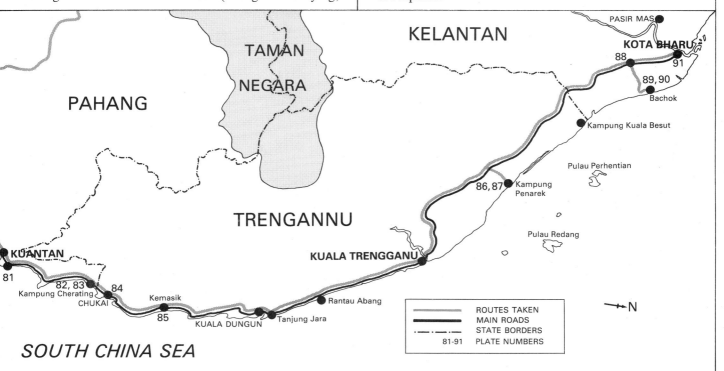

PLATE 86   PAGE 79

Beyond Kuala Trengganu the road swings inland and then runs northwest, parallel with the coast. Following a hunch, I took a twenty-kilometre diversion to the sea and the village of Kampung Penarek, and was rewarded with this typical array of fish laid out on platforms of split bamboo above the high-tide mark.

It was Friday, an hour or so after midday. The sun reached its zenith, and the otherwise quiet village swarmed with colour as men gathered for the

PLATE 87   PAGES 12-13

essential *hari juma'at* (Friday) prayers. Muslims are expected to pray five times a day, and this obeisance to Allah can be performed anywhere. But on Fridays, attendance at noon prayers is compulsory. This is a time when everyone wears his "Friday best" — a freshly washed sarong, a bright *baju* (shirt), and the black velvet cap known as a *songkok*; unless you have made the *haj* (pilgrimage) to the holy city of Mecca, which entitles you to the white skull-cap and the honorific of *Haji*. Every Muslim aspires to (and is expected to) make the *haj* at least once in a lifetime, and thousands of Malaysians take the long voyage or flight to Saudi Arabia every year. Trengganu and Kelantan are particular strongholds of orthodox Islam, as the number of white-capped men and boys in this photograph makes clear.

I had talked to a number of the men before prayers began, and had asked if they'd mind my taking a photograph. Some of the older men demurred; the middle-aged were intrigued, and agreed; the young took advantage of my adequate but not very good Bahasa Malaysia, and scoffed at this stranger from outer space; while the boys (as ever) thought the whole thing was a marvellous joke. Then, while they were all in the *masjid*, I downed a plate of *nasi goreng* (fried rice) and a couple of glasses of soya-bean milk *pakai air batu* (with ice). Later, having set up the camera, I sat on the steps of the mosque amid a hundred pairs of shoes and sandals. The prayers and sermon finished. Bodies flowed out of the mosque like a tidal wave. A flurry of hand signals. Utter stillness. And finally, the faint click of the shuttter.

Within a stone's throw of the Kelantan border I stopped at a tiny roadside stall for a durian, the "king of fruits". They were being sold in fours or fives. Fine. I sat on the wooden platform (shoes off, of course), and watched a first offering being prised open with a short *parang*. Satisfactory, not outstanding. I asked an old man on the platform to recommend the next fruit. He looked, shook, listened, smelled. "*Biji ini* — this one." Magnificent! As was his next recommendation. What does a durian taste like? I'm afraid the English language just doesn't have enough words relating to taste, smell or texture to do justice to this extraordinary fruit. In any case, I'm totally and happily addicted — I love it with a passion, and am

always amazed that so many newcomers find its odour offensive and its texture slimy. *Chacun à son goût.*

Also close to the border, at Jerteh, is the turn-off to Kampung Kuala Besut, where you can hire boats for the twenty-kilometre journey to the islands of Perhentian, certainly among the more lovely of those gracing the east coast. This group has not yet been developed for tourism (in itself, an attraction for some travellers), and an overnight stay is best accomplished under canvas, though there's a small rest house with very limited accommodation.

Not far from Kota Bharu is the modern Istana Negeri Kelantan, the "palace of the state of Kelantan", with immaculate gardens and lawns that seem to have been

PLATE 88   PAGE 137

trimmed with nail clippers. The gatehouse reflects the design of the main palace complex, a monumental and pleasing blend of traditional Islamic architecture and up-to-the-minute engineering in pre-stressed concrete — in a way, a symbol of the blend of old and new that makes Malaysia such an engrossing experience. The spirit, if not the substance, of ancient styles and traditions survives here in some of the most lovely and adventurous architecture to be seen anywhere.

I took another of my seaward diversions just south of Kota Bharu. This time my objective was the holiday and resort area of Bachok, highly popular with local people (one obvious reason: an abundance of *makan* and drink stalls, enveloped by stationary fleets of small motorcycles while the region's bikies restore themselves with lip-smackin' stall food).

Yet just beyond the red plastic buckets and permanently erected steel umbrellas was the vista of the older and seemingly indestructible east coast. North and

PLATE 89   PAGES 76-77

south, as far as the eye could see, were squadrons of small boats, stranded above the tide mark of shell fragments and pieces of driftwood.

To the southeast, a distant storm was herding its clouds, dropping its cargo of moisture in sheets of silvery light (the edges of such falls are frequently so well defined that you can be on a wet road at one second, on a dry road the next).

I was about two kilometres up the road from Bachok. Out to sea, perhaps two hundred metres

PLATE 90   PAGE 78

offshore, a lone *perahu* was moving slowly in to the beach. While I was setting up this shot of a *bangau* (spar-rest) with its flat "shadow puppet" figures of *Ramayana* characters — now seen less and less on east coast boats — the ten-metre fishing boat ground its prow into the sand. Poles were slung across the thwarts; shoulders of a dozen stalwart men moved under the poles; wooden rollers lined the path up the beach from the boat's prow. The usual business of heaving a heavy boat above the high-tide mark, an everyday event; and suddenly I was part of it.

Well, it's hard to resist. In bare feet, I'm just eight centimetres short of two metres (six feet four inches in pre-metric days). Reasonably healthy. And a giant by Malaysian standards. So, here was a friendly giant, here was a boat that had to be hauled, here were fifty encouraging young fans, none of them old or tall enough to get a shoulder within a metre of the cross-poles. I couldn't let them down, could I? Having survived the experience, I merely recommend that if you're ever asked to help shoulder a boat onto the high, dry sand — don't! It's punishing work, and I have nothing but admiration for the men who do it, day in, day out, as simply a part of their livelihood.

The end of my peninsular travel was approaching. At Kota Bharu, there would be a halt, a time for reflection. Time to buy a rail ticket back to Singapore, to see the BMW wheeled into a goodsvan and securely roped. Why didn't I just jump on the bike and ride the nine hundred kilometres? Because, even on an assignment, I ride for pleasure, and there's not much pleasure to be obtained in racing down highways in a desperate attempt to get from point A to point B in X number of hours. What's more, I share Paul Theroux's liking for trains, and the eighteen-hour journey was something to look forward to. I had a sleeper, and the restaurant car would be well-stocked with *mee goreng*, *nasi goreng* and cold beer. What more could a tired traveller ask for?

PLATE 91   PAGE 4

Meantime, I had an overnight stay in KB, a big, sprawling, bustling city with not much charm but a great deal of exuberant vitality — and that can be charm enough.

I needed some symbol of *jalan-jalan*, and I found it here, close to the vast central market. The trishaw appears in many forms in many Malaysian towns and cities, and is used for a myriad purposes: regular transport, a taste of something different for tourists, a sort of ferry service for getting two or three children to and from school, a carrier of cargo and market goods. I like to think I can carry a lot on the BMW; compared with the loads that are pedalled on trishaws, I'm just beginning. And there are local distinguishing features. In Pinang, the passenger seats are in front of the rider; here, in Kota Bharu, they run a Singapore-style outfit — but so much more ornate!

Borneo! Oh, the visions that name evokes — especially among people who've never been there. Residents of Sarawak, Sabah and Indonesian Kalimantan may view it somewhat differently, but there can't be many Westerners who haven't thrilled to *Boys' Own Paper* (or its equivalent) stories of White Rajahs, head-hunters, long-houses, Dyaks, foaming rivers, dense jungle, blow-pipes, and adventures that would be totally out of the question anywhere else in the world. Twenty-five-metre pythons who kill their prey with poisonous breath; carnivorous plants who relish a hunter

for dinner; swamps inhabited by loathsome creatures that make a dinosaur look like a household pet.

Well, yes and no. A young English adventurer by the name of James Brooke *did* become Rajah of Sarawak in 1841, establishing a benevolent if paternalistic dynasty that ruled until 1946. Almost forty years after Brooke's "accession", the territory now known as Sabah was ceded to an Austro-Hungarian baron and the scion of a long-established trading company in Hong Kong. (Part of the allure of Borneo is that its actual history is more fanciful than anything conjured up by a writer of fiction.) And there are pythons, though seldom more than six metres in length; and they certainly don't *breathe* people to death — like most jungle creatures, they shun human contact, and they attack nothing larger than a chicken or small goat.

Blow-pipes are still used for hunting by some of the inland tribespeople; and the last human heads were taken during the dark days of World War II. Carnivorous plants? Omniverous is a better description: they digest anything, if it's small enough; but they know that eating people is wrong — thrust your finger down the throat of a pitcher-plant, and you'll retrieve it in one piece, without so much as a tooth mark.

The mist of myth, legend and hearsay is quickly dispelled in Borneo's major towns: Kuching, Sibu, Miri, Kota Kinabalu. All of them riverine or coastal towns (river and sea are still economic lifelines here; rivers especially are highways to up-country settlements and long-houses), all of them combining

PLATE 92   PAGES 84-85

twentieth-century commercial activity and bustle with touches of a more sedate, traditional way of life — among the pale-skinned Europeans in a supermarket you might rub shoulders with a tattooed Iban or a Kenyah woman with ear-lobes stretched by heavy brass weights.

Or in Kuching on a Friday, your vantage point being a high-rise building, you can watch the swirl of

PLATE 93   PAGES 124-125

movement as the mosque empties after noonday prayers. In Sibu, which I travelled to by high-powered motorboat through coastal waters from Kuching (such boats being the Borneo equivalent of an out-station taxi), I found this market. Throbbing, vital, and in many respects more important than the markets on the peninsula, because here the customer is not just a townsman or woman dropping in for daily needs — here there is also the once-a-month buyer come down from the rivers, from the hills, with a shopping list that includes such essentials of frontier life as nails, wire, drums of kerosene, a hundred kilos of rice, a new *parang*. The large towns of Sarawak and Sabah support and are supported by their immediate population. They are also supply bases, on a scale unknown in Peninsular Malaysia. For many up-country people, a monthly or yearly visit to such towns is a major event, an expedition involving perhaps several days of travel.

There is money, too, for frivolous, ephemeral pur-

PLATE 94   PAGES 120-121

chases. It would be hard to pass by this display in Sibu and not be tempted to lash out on something guaranteed to last for at least ten minutes in the hands of a reasonably sensible child.

Sibu is pretty much the end of the road as far as four-wheeled traffic is concerned. For the really dedicated traveller who doesn't mind roughing it, it's also a gateway to some magnificent river and jungle trips. Equipped with small-format cameras, I've done some of those trips; with the bulk of the 8 × 10, I wouldn't consider it.

I took the logical and easy way out of Sibu by flying to Miri. My goal was the Niah Caves, a highpoint for anyone visiting Sarawak — not a magic-carpet ride, but

PLATE 95   PAGE 148

worth ten times the effort involved in getting there.

Be prepared for a two-hour drive to Batu Niah, a forty-five-minute cruise upstream in a powered longboat, and a further hour's hike along a narrow board-walk (the planks aren't there for eager tourists, they simply make life easier for people who earn a living by digging out guano — bat droppings — and carrying it to the outside world where it is highly valued as a fertiliser). The caves themselves defy description. You can play with words like awesome, staggering, monumental, inspiring, majestic . . .

PLATE 96   PAGES 152-153

yet even in combination they don't get close to summing up the vastness of this rock-enclosed space.

The "Great Cave" has been photographed thousands of times. I've yet to see a print or a transparency that really conveys its scale. Those spindly spider-web poles reaching to the ceiling are sixty or seventy metres high and are climbed by gatherers of swifts' nests, the basic ingredient in "birds' nest soup". The main cavern and its neighbours are inhabited by tens of thousands of bats and birds, and were also the shelter, about forty thousand years ago, for some of the earliest known forms of *Homo sapiens*.

Even in these days of multi-national corporations, it is hard to imagine one company owning a single block of real estate covering seventy-five thousand square kilometres. The British North Borneo Company did, when it controlled what is now Sabah.

I flew into the capital, Kota Kinabalu, with one goal in mind: to haul the 8 × 10 to the top of Gunung Kina-

balu, at four thousand and forty metres the highest mountain in Southeast Asia. Having done the climb before, and knowing just how gruelling it can be, I

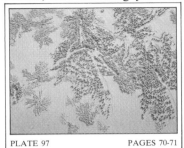

PLATE 97   PAGES 70-71

was easily diverted to KK's lovely beaches, and to Tanjung Aru in particular.

Small sand-carrying crabs are found on most of Malaysia's beaches. The patterns they create with their activity are works of art (if crabs can be artists). Having set up the camera for this shot, I waited for about ten minutes until a couple of the sand-carriers

PLATE 98   PAGE 72

recovered from my intrusion and emerged from the shelter of their holes. Farther down the same beach some children were performing acrobatics. I lined them up for a long shot, and just hoped that something interesting might happen. It did. Purely by chance the backward somersault and the appearance of the horse and rider coincided.

This and the following shot are about as close to an unposed "candid" as it's possible to get with an 8 × 10 in the field, though being far enough away to be inconspicuous means having to sacrifice any hope of a close-up. However, a compensation is the achievement of a point of view that seems almost detached from the subject—somewhat akin to looking through the wrong end of a telescope.

It seems that everybody in KK is a jogger. That's the

PLATE 99   PAGE 73

impression I got. No matter where I looked along the beach, there was sure to be somebody exercising lungs and heart and muscles in the sea air.

Sunset, and a slow shutter speed, an attractive combination if you're aiming for a sense of movement.

This was not a difficult shot. There were so many runners that it was just a matter of time before I found a subject; the tricky bit was calculating precisely when they were in front of the lens.

And so to the mountain. It has been scaled and de-

PLATE 100   PAGES 166-167

scended (base camp to summit to base camp) in less than twelve hours — not a feat I would recommend. This view from Kinabalu National Park explains why: there's a lot of ground to cover. Most people do the return trip in two days, and end up with painfully aching muscles as a result. Far better to allow yourself three days; the first to climb from the power station above the base camp to Panar

Laban Hut, the second (with a start very early in the morning) to reach the summit and return to the hut; the third to ease your screaming muscles with a leisurely descent to the base camp. If you need any more convincing, just have a look at fellow climbers returning to base after the two-day marathon!

Another point worth remembering is that the trail itself is probably the mountain's major attraction. Attaining the peak provides a feeling of achievement and satisfaction; but the peak ought not to be your sole aim, for there is so much to be savoured on the way up. At the lower levels, the atmosphere is hot and humid; you're climbing tree-trunk staircases amid a tangle of vines and jungly growth. Higher up, there's the more sparse vegetation of montane forest and a glorious mini-world to be explored. Here is where you'll find masses of pitcher plants.

PLATE 101   PAGE 150

I was precariously balanced on a spongy bank of moss in taking this close-up, and I needed a long exposure. It must have been my lucky day, for a fly settled inside the lip of the pitcher just as I had finished calculating the aperture and shutter speed. Little did it realise that it was doomed!

PLATE 102   PAGE 149

I could easily have spent days taking shots of this wonderfully varied scene. There was so much to examine in detail, so many small plants and blooms of glorious shape and texture, a feeling of organic richness that was quite overwhelming.

I am told there are more than a thousand species of orchids and mosses in the Park. It's not hard to believe. Nor am I surprised that amateur botanists sometimes fail to make the peak — they become so

PLATE 103   PAGE 151

engrossed in the vegetation all around them that they practically need to be hog-tied and carried off the slopes.

Just look at this parasite. Is it a living plant, or a piece of wire sculpture? The answer doesn't matter — what is so compelling is its intricate form, its delicacy.

As you climb higher you enter a silvery forest of gnarled and stunted growth, a dramatic contrast after the rain forest of the lower slopes.

This is not, perhaps, the sort of vegetation you expect so close to the equator. It has none of the softness and almost animal pliancy of huge-leafed jungle plants; now there is a sparse, stringy toughness.

PLATE 104   PAGES 168-169

This is the scene about ten minutes away from the hut from which, in the dark hours of early morning, you begin your final ascent.

Here you're more than three thousand metres above sea level, and the temperature is hardly what you'd expect in the tropics. Looking back from Panar Laban Hut, you'll find this magnificent vista of ridges and gullies; you're not yet at the top, but you begin to realise why the journey itself is so rewarding.

PLATE 105   PAGES 174-175

Soon the vegetation disappears completely, and you're faced with a huge dome of gran-

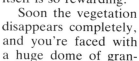

	ROADS
	AIR
	BOAT
	STATE BORDERS
	NATIONAL BORDERS
92-107	PLATE NUMBERS

SOUTH CHINA SEA

KOTA BELUD

Gunung Kinabalu
101,102,103,104,105, 106,107

KOTA KINABALU
97,98,99

SANDAKAN

BRUNEI

MIRI

SABAH

Niah Caves
95,96

LAHAD DATU

SEMPORNA

TAWAU

SIBU
93,94

92
KUCHING

SARAWAK

KALIMANTAN

N

ite dominating your horizon. Where are Borneo's golden beaches and softly swaying palms? Not here, certainly, in this harsh, forbidding landscape; not here, among this desolate bleakness. Small wonder that the mountain is held in awe by the people of the plains and rivers.

Finally, the summit. Rock, nothing but rock. And views to take your breath away (if you have any left to spare after the climb).

This is perhaps the time to contemplate

PLATE 106   PAGES 170-171

PLATE 107   PAGES 172-173

the richness and magic of Malaysia, to relish images of the places you've seen and the people you've met.

From your vantage point on top of the world, with the mighty drop of Low's Gully falling away below, you can also sketch in your mind's eye a whole new series of adventures on the road, and perhaps look forward to other times when you'll be captured by the joys of going *jalan-jalan* in Malaysia.

The camera

This short section is not intended to be an instruction manual on the use of an 8 × 10 studio camera (or "view camera", to be more accurate) in the field. Anything I can say to view-camera photographers won't be news. But for the millions who use small-format "automatic" cameras these days, it might suggest that there's a lot more to view-camera photography than "just point and shoot".

The 8 × 10 Deardorff is big and heavy. It has been hand-crafted from start to finish. It is a magnificent piece of finely tuned machinery. And in using such a superb beast there is, in some ways, a regression; turning back the clock almost a century and a half to the beginnings of photography.

The earliest cameras were simply an application of the principle of the *camera obscura* (a "darkened room") — light penetrating a small hole in one wall of the room would throw an inverted, upside-down image

Under the viewing hood one hundred years ago.

on the opposite wall. If that opposite wall could be thinly coated with a layer of light-sensitive chemical solution such as silver oxide, then a permanent imprint of the image was possible. The room became a small box, the chemical coating and its necessary fixatives were gradually perfected, and the world was introduced to photography. All view cameras follow that basic principle — the "hole" is a lens, the "opposite wall" is a sheet of film.

Simple. So is the theory of operation. The lens at the front of the box transmits the image to the "opposite

wall", which is the sheet of film. How does the photographer view the subject through the lens? Again, simple. Before the film-holder is slid into place, the photographer can see the image on a ground-glass plate at the back of the camera — although that image is inverted and upside-down, everything seen there will also be seen on the final negative or positive. This is the time for focus adjustment, for correction of perspective (a factor I'll return to in a moment), for composition and framing. Everything ready? OK. Close the lens, insert the film-holder, remove the black slide in front of the film sheet, and open the lens at the aperture and shutter-speed desired.

The complications arise with the features that give a view camera its advantages. The advantages are the built-in bellows controlling focus, coupled to the front and back ends of a body that is not rigid — the lens-board and the film-back can move up, down, or sideways; front (lens) and back (film) can be twisted through a vertical axis; and all of these variations can be done independently of each other. As a result, the photographer can control horizontal and vertical perspective, and also the plane of focus. With anything other than a view camera, this can only be achieved with "optional extras". Now for the complications.

There are four possible movements with the 8 × 10 Deardorff. **1. Rise and fall** of front or back, which lets you position the subject at the centre, top or bottom of the film sheet with almost no change of perspective (and that only when the front is moved). **2. Shift**, involving sideways movement of the front or back of the camera, and which positions the subject at the centre, left or right of the film. **3. Tilt**, in which movement of the back changes the subject's perspective, and movement of the front changes the point of focus. **4. Swing**, with the back or front being "swung" left or right on a vertical axis — back-swing changing perspective, front-swing changing the direction of focus from straight in front of the camera to a fairly narrow "corridor" left or right of the subject.

Of these four basic options, "tilt" and "swing" are generally the most important because of the effect they have on focus. Taken in combination — tilt, swing, shift, and rise or fall, plus the backward-forward movements of the bellows — the variations are virtually limitless. All they need is time!

Another factor is the choice of apertures available. I carried three lenses: 121 mm f/8, 300 mm f/5.6, and 480 mm f/9 (equivalent, respectively, to 21 mm, 50 mm and 80 mm with a 35-millimetre camera). The fastest lens was the 300 mm f/5.6, but it has a limited depth of field — at f/16 I could only achieve a depth of field from twelve metres to infinity, compared with three metres to infinity with the equivalent 35-millimetre lens. Of course, with manipulation of the front and back of the camera I could get sharper focus closer to the lens, but only after a lot of twiddling with knurled knobs and screws. Not as simple as one or two changes on a barrel lens.

Working with Kodak Ektachrome rated at ASA 64, and given the slow lenses (a standard 50 mm at f/5.6!!), I found that even in sunny conditions I was shooting at around one-eighth of a second with the lens wide open. On a setting of f/32 or f/64, quite often needed for greater depth of field, I was beginning to think in terms of seconds and even minutes. The need for a strong tripod was obvious.

The disciplines involved in view-camera photography are very different from those encountered with 35-millimetre cameras, and there are also differences between 8 × 10 and smaller view-camera formats. Patience becomes a special virtue: the setting up of a large, heavy camera, the intricacies of focussing, swinging, tilting. And you have to learn to be sparing with film. Every sheet costs about the same as two rolls of 35-millimetre Ektachrome, and one sheet means one shot. Inevitably, there's more planning, more care. The ideal situation is to be able to set up the subject (and to direct it, if it's a human subject), open the shutter, and then hit the road again. That's ideal; it doesn't happen all that often.

There can be other problems as well. I had my film processed after one trip, and was dismayed to find some pinkish-gold splotches on a few of the transparencies. Either a needle-hole light leak in the bellows or the changing bag. It turned out to be a miniscule hole in the

changing bag. From then on, I discarded the bag. Whenever I wanted to replenish the film-holders (I carried five, equal to ten shots, with additional raw film in the bag above the petrol tank), I sought out the nearest commercial photographic studio in the nearest medium-sized town. "May I use your darkroom . . . ?" "*Boleh*. OK!" From that time onward, no more problems with light leaks.

Care and attention pay off. I had a success ratio of about 1:2.5 or better, as opposed to the roughly 1:10 I would hope for (as really good shots, not merely passable ones) in shooting 35-mm.

Would I do it again? Of course. Though next time I'm going to try hand-holding, with a fixed focus . . . .

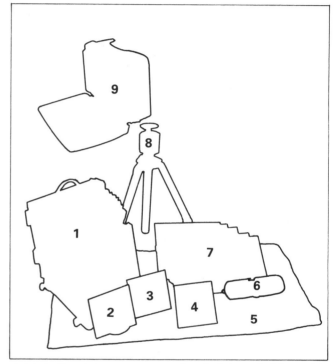

A key to the plate on PAGE 176 — the whole box of tricks, and its conveyance. **1.** 8 × 10 camera body by L.F. Deardorff & Sons, Inc., Chicago, Illinois, USA; serial number 5414. **2.** Lens by Rodenstock: Apo-Ronar, Copal No. 3, 1:9/480 mm. **3.** Lens by Schneider-Kreuznach: Symmar S, Copal No. 3, 1:5.6/300 mm. **4.** Lens by Schneider-Kreuznach: Super-Angulon, 1:8/121 mm. **5.** Viewing hood. **6.** Lightmeter by Gossen: Lunasix 3. **7.** Five film-holders by Kodak. **8.** Tripod by Gizo: Tele Studex 502/4; and ball-head by Lumpf. **9.** Saddlebag by BMW, with specially modified interior to hold lenses and film-holders; the matching saddlebag modified to hold the folded camera body.

On the road in Malaysia

I wouldn't mind a dollar for every time I saw that signal. It might be a pedestrian, another motorcyclist, the driver of a car or truck. Not that it mattered. The signal was always the same: a hand held forwards and horizontally, fingers and thumb snapping open and shut like a duck's beak. Always in broad daylight, always with the same meaning: "Hey, mister, your lights are on!"

Yes, of course they were on. For me, a first rule of the road in Malaysia — be visible. This is not a lecture on road safety or a plea for good-mannered motorists,

but as someone who's driven from Europe to East Asia I can assure you that a motorbike with its headlights on (during the day) is far more easily seen than one with headlights doused.

Malaysia's road system varies from adequate to excellent, with most of it being good; in fact, it's surprising how many apparently minor back roads are asphalted. Nonetheless, there are traps for the unwary motorist, and even more for the unwary motorcyclist. The road surface *can* be uneven (especially after the monsoon season); small dirt side roads, leading from logging camps or plantations to a main highway, often mean a slick of slippery laterite or clay on the trunk route's bitumen; in rural areas especially, people and domestic animals — mostly goats or cows — regard the road as a communal pathway; and there are many, many sharp or blind corners at the end of fairly straight stretches of road.

Rain is also a hazard. For one thing, tropical downpours tend to be regional rather than general — a dry road one minute, a wet one the next, sometimes with deep puddles that can send you into an out-of-control slalom. It's never a joy to drive *in* the rain, but by keeping a weather-eye open you can see the clouds lighten from black to deep purple to silvery grey, and know you've got five minutes to take shelter.

Tens of thousands of Malaysians drive motorbikes. They're mostly louder on noise than big on performance. One reason I like the BMW is that it tends to drive itself; for such a big bike, it's not too heavy; and its horizontal pistons give it a low centre of gravity and greater stability. I mention this because motorcycling (or *travelling* by motorbike) should be enjoyable. A good bike, well balanced, gives you the chance to look at the landscape — certainly, you don't have to spend quite so much time with your eyes glued to the road in front of you as you would with a lighter, less stable machine.

So, a few tips. Headlights on, even in daylight. A strong horn to give plenty of warning of your approach.

Effective rear-vision mirrors so that you know as much about what's happening behind you as you do about what's happening in front. Strong shoes or boots (I wear US Army jungle issue) for those times when you need a trailing foot — or when you simply want to get off the road and walk into some exquisite patch of jungle that's caught your eye.

Assuming you're travelling for pleasure, and not just for the sake of getting from one point to another in the shortest possible time, never drive for more than an hour or so without a break. On the one hand, I find this keeps me more relaxed; on the other, it's an opportunity to nip into a coffee shop for coffee or a bite to eat, and another chance to make contact with people. With so many motorcyclists in Malaysia, I invariably attracted hordes of curious, friendly onlookers — and the inevitable questions about price, size of engine, and miles per gallon. Good conversation starters. And they always want to know where you're coming from, and where you're going. Breaks the ice.

Be careful of the sun. Even on hazy days, the equatorial sunlight can burn you to a blister. Equip yourself with plenty of anti-sunburn cream for arms and hands; wear long-sleeved shirts if you prefer. The heat on a sunny day might make you forget about the chill-factor of wind, but *don't* forget — your slipstream wind, whipping past your kidneys and a shirt that is sure to be damp with perspiration, can create problems. I always wear a scarf or sarong tied around my midriff on hot days, especially on a long-distance ride. And don't omit regular drinks to replace the body moisture lost through perspiration.

The other protection needed is for head and face. A crash-helmet, of course; and preferably with a clear, untinted plastic visor — an insect (built like a miniature bomber) in the eye is no way to enjoy life on the open road.

Biography of a book

Few writers, illustrators or photographers ever enjoy the opportunity (and challenge) of designing and producing the book that enshrines their work; few of them, I guess, would even want the challenge, though many must wonder just what happens to their *oeuvre* after it leaves their hands for those of a publisher. Having been the victim, on occasion, of bad printing myself, I can sympathise only too readily with their anguish when the final result is not up to expectations — mediocre typesetting, poor quality binding, out-of-register colours.

I'm fortunate in being able to control most of those factors; or, at least, to minimise the chance of anything going wrong. Trained in book production, typesetting, printing and design, I can not only envisage how a book will look, but also know how best to achieve the quality and finish desired.

The mechanics of bookmaking have seen more revolutionary changes in the last ten years than they have since Gutenberg's day — typesetting on film, laser scanners for colour separations, high-speed four-colour presses. Yet the *art* of bookmaking remains constant. Typefaces, paper, binding — these, and many other

factors, still have to be selected with great care and imagination.

As a photographer, I regard the colour reproduction of a photograph on a sheet of paper as an integral part of photography, as an extension of the image captured in chemicals adhering to a sheet of celluloid. The means of transferring the image from the original film to printing plates is therefore of the utmost importance.

The sharpness of the image in 8×10 transparencies demands the most sophisticated colour-separation techniques in order to minimise loss of detail (there is always a small percentage loss in any mechanical reproduction). The best equipment currently available is the laser scanner, in which a computer-controlled beam of light is used to break down the colour image into four components: magenta (red), cyan (blue), yellow and black. Each component thus "separated" appears on film as a fine mesh of tiny dots, varying in size according to the intensity of the colour at any particular point. The number of dots in one linear inch (2.54 centimetres) is known as the "screen", and the higher the screen number the finer will be the quality of reproduction — *if* the paper is right. I chose 170-screen for *jalan-jalan*, which is very fine, but quite hopeless on anything other than a very smooth paper with a very hard finish.

The laser scanner in question is a Hell DC 300 ER, operated by Colourscan in Singapore, and capable of producing separations up to a size slightly larger than this book when opened flat. Using the computer, I was able to select my own settings for colour values in the separation process.

Excellent colour separations are one thing. Inks and paper are another, for these two must be of the highest quality if fine reproduction is to be obtained. The body of the book, including the endpapers, is printed in DIC Super Highgloss four-colour process ink on 150-gram Japanese art paper coated on both sides; 120-gram art paper has been used on the covers; and the cover boards are 32-ounce Strawboard made by Singapore Paper Products.

Typesetting is also a critical factor in the making of any book. Type should not only be easy to read; it should also complement the tone of the book and its accompanying illustrations so that the overall character of the end product is harmonious and aesthetically pleasing.

For headings and body text I selected Times New Roman, a twentieth-century typeface modelled on the classical faces of the eighteenth century — elegant, yet easy to read. Setting for the foreword and section introductions was done by Quality Typesetting, Singapore, on a Monophoto 1000 Model 400/8; while the commentary and notes were photoset by Polyglot, Singapore, on a Linotron 202; all body text is ten points, leaded one point. The typeface used in the maps in this section is Univers, also photoset by Polyglot.

The book was printed by Koon Wah Printing, Singapore, in the four-colour offset lithography process on a Heidelberg Speedmaster press.

Further reading

Fact, it is true, is sometimes stranger than fiction; on the other hand, the presentation of factual material can often be extremely dull, a mere recital of dates, names and events with little feeling for people and places. But the same material, handled with skill by a perceptive, sympathetic novelist, can be made to come alive.

In those terms, there are two works of fiction I have long thought ought to be compulsory reading for anyone visiting Malaysia. Both of them powerfully and accurately evoke aspects of Malaysian life and people that were true in the past, and are true today — not perhaps the whole truth, but so close to it that the discrepancies hardly matter.

Henri Fauconnier's *Soul of Malaya* won the Prix Goncourt in 1930, and was translated into English in 1931. Set on the east coast of the peninsula, it is probably the most haunting and evocative book ever written with Malaysia as a background. It has recently been re-issued as an Oxford in Asia Paperback.

The second, Anthony Burgess' *The Malayan Trilogy* (Penguin), is full of wry, penetrating observations, and is often uproariously funny; but beneath the sometimes raunchy humour there is a real feeling for Malaysian small-town life.

A third novel of less literary merit, but of interest because of its portrait of the culture and people of Kelantan, is G.M. Glaskin's *The Beach of Passionate Love*.

Somewhat dated, but still worth reading for occasional flashes of pertinent observation on the old "Malayan" scene, are the beautifully written and delightfully bitchy *Malayan Stories* of W. Somerset Maugham. The stories scandalised white colonial society, who felt they were being harshly portrayed — or were too easily recognisable!

Reminiscent of Maugham, and just as readable, is Paul Theroux's recently published collection of short stories, *The Consul's File* (Penguin).

I should also recommend anything you can get hold of by Lat. Lat is a young Malay cartoonist who, in the last four years, has won the loyalty of tens of thousands of fans for his stunningly accurate (and *very* funny) renderings of life in the *kampung*, the town, the city — *Lat's Lot*, *Lots of Lat* and *With a Little Bit of Lat* are three of his collections that spring to mind, and there are others.

Two very good histories, well informed but not too academic for the general reader, are Harry Miller's *The Story of Malaysia* and Victor Purcell's *Malaysia*. Miller is a former editor of the *Straits Times*; Purcell was a member of the Malayan Civil Service. A detailed history of the extraordinary Brooke dynasty is Steven Runciman's *The White Rajahs: a History of Sarawak from 1841 to 1946*.

The culture of Malaysia has been increasingly well covered in recent years. Two excellent and well illustrated books are Mubin Sheppard's *Taman Indera: Malay Decorative Arts and Pastimes* (Oxford University Press) and *Living Crafts of Malaysia* (Times Books International). Also worth reading, though a little pedantic at times, is N.J. Ryan's *The Cultural Heritage of Malaya* (Longman).

Personal memoirs are often a good source of information about a country. At the top of my list is Isabella Bird's *The Golden Chersonese*, an account of travels in the peninsula at a time when the first British

Residents were being appointed (a hundred years ago, few men had ventured where this intrepid woman travelled). Also good, though dry in parts, are Sir Frank Swettenham's *Malayan Journals 1874–1876*. In more recent years there have been F. Spencer Chapman's *The Jungle is Neutral*, a harrowing story of three years behind enemy lines during World War II; Tom Harrison's *World Within: a Borneo Story* and Malcolm MacDonald's *Borneo People*, both of which deal colourfully and extensively with Sarawak; and Charles Shuttleworth's *Malayan Safari*, the fascinating story of a former game warden, hunter and guide.

The books listed here are a personal choice. They have all provided me with information, or enjoyment, or both. Needless to say, there are many others to be found if you browse through major bookstores in Kuala Lumpur or Singapore, or if you're interested enough to check out the catalogue in your local library.

Finally, the Insight Guide, *Malaysia* (APA Productions, sixth edition, 1980) is to be recommended as a highly informative introduction to Malaysian culture, history, lifestyle and people, as well as being a colourful, up-to-date handbook on what to do and where to go.

Acknowledgements

If I had sought the name of every person who befriended or aided me in the course of my going *jalan-jalan* through Malaysia, this brief section would look more like a telephone directory than a few words of thanks. In all the thousands of kilometres that I travelled, I cannot ever remember being greeted with hostility or suspicion— as a sort of travelling one-man circus, yes, but anyone doing what I was doing would have to expect that, anywhere.

So, first of all, I must say *terima kasih* (thank you) to the hundreds of Malaysians, in the *kampung* or in the city, who helped make my journey such a pleasurable experience. Two groups of people deserve special praise: the coffee-shop and *makan*-stall proprietors who fed me so well, and the owners of photographic studios who let me into darkrooms to change film.

I am also extremely grateful to the Tourist Development Corporation (TDC), Malaysia, for not only encouraging me to pursue this project, but for making financially possible the publication of this first edition. For their advice and assistance I am particularly indebted to the director general and deputy director general of TDC, Datuk Baharuddin Musa and Encik Abdullah Jonid.

Closer to home, I owe many thanks to Kodak Singapore for processing the exposed film; to Colourscan for the interest, goodwill and overtime they put into perfecting the colour separations; to Quality Typesetting and Polyglot for their typesetting; to Koon Wah Printing for their printing; and to Tony Khoo for his maps.

On a more personal level, four special acknowledgements: Leo Haks, whose imagination and energy got this book off the ground in the first place; Lat, the incomparable cartoonist whose ingenious and sympathetic work was a constant source of inspiration; Idanna Pucci, for her limitless patience; and Peter Hutton, who undertook the task of interpreting my travel notes and tapes.

My colleagues at Apa Productions deserve special mention for their invaluable support. It would be invidious to single out individual contributions when so much effort was put into so many different tasks — but to Leonard Lueras, Ian Lloyd, Alice Ng, Raymond Boey, William Tjoeng, Molly Wee, Ivy Tan and Peter Wee, my gratitude.

The last page. The journey is almost over. An appropriate time, I think, to remember BMW and Deardorff, without whom . . . Before too long, I hope, we'll be going *jalan-jalan* together once more.